PRACTICAL SOCIAL WORK

Series Editor: Jo Campling

(BASW)

Social work is at an important stage in its development. All professions must be responsive to changing social and economic conditions if they are to meet the needs of those they serve. This series focuses on sound practice and the specific contribution which social workers can make to the well-being of our society in the 1980s.

The British Association of Social Workers has always been conscious of its role in setting guidelines for practice and in seeking to raise professional standards. The conception of the Practical Social Work series arose from a survey of BASW members to discover where they, the practitioners in social work, felt there was the most need for new literature. The response was overwhelming and enthusiastic, and the result is a carefully planned, coherent series of books. The emphasis is firmly on practice, set in a theoretical framework. The books will inform, stimulate and promote discussion, thus adding to the further development of skills and high professional standards. All the authors are practitioners and teachers of social work, representing a wide variety of experience.

JO CAMPLING

PRACTICAL SOCIAL WORK

Series Editor: Jo Campling

BASW

PUBLISHED

Social Work and Mental Handicap
David Anderson

Residential Work
Roger Clough

Social Work with Old People
Mary Marshall

Social Work with Disabled People
Michael Oliver

Working in Teams
Malcolm Payne

Social Work with the Dying and Bereaved
Carole R. Smith

Community Work
Alan Twelvetrees

FORTHCOMING

Social Work with Ethnic Minorities
Alun Jackson

Applied Psychology for Social Workers
Paula Nicolson and Rowan Bayne

Social Work with the Mentally Ill
Colin Pritchard and Alan Butler

Social Work with Juvenile Offenders
David Thorpe, Norman Tutt, David Smith and
Christopher Green

Social Work and Mental Handicap

David Anderson

MACMILLAN

First published 1982
Reprinted 1985

Published by
MACMILLAN EDUCATION LTD
Houndmills, Basingstoke, Hampshire RG21 2XS
and London
Companies and representatives
throughout the world

Printed in Hong Kong

ISBN 0–333–32702–0 (hardcover)
ISBN 0–333–32703–9 (paperback)

Contents

Acknowledgements

I have had a great deal of help and support in preparing this book from friends, parents, teachers, social workers and voluntary workers. Its faults would be far more numerous without them. I have been greatly heartened every time I have talked with mentally handicapped people themselves, because of their rich humanity and warmth. They have far more to give than they take, and I hope this book may encourage one or two more people to join the struggle to open for them their proper place in our society. Irene, my wife, has helped with it at every stage, kept me human when she could, and pushed me when I felt defeated by my handicaps.

Cambridge   DAVID ANDERSON
January 1982

List of Abbreviations

ATC	Adult Training Centre
CCETSW	Central Council for Education and Training in Social Work
CMH	Campaign for Mentally Handicapped People
ESN/M	Educationally Subnormal/Mild
ESN/S	Educationally Subnormal/Severe
MENCAP	see NSMHC
MIND NAMH	National Association for Mental Health
NSMHC	National Society for Mentally Handicapped Children and Adults
NSPCC	National Society for the Prevention of Cruelty to Children
PASS	Programme Analysis of Service Systems
SSD	Social Services Department

Introduction

The last ten years have seen a revolution in thinking about mentally handicapped people. A glance at any bibliography shows what a volume of new thinking was generated in the 1970s. Of course pioneers like Jack Tizard and Albert Kushlick were pointing the way in the 1960s, but their work — establishing principles, creating models, and planning comprehensive systems of service — came into its own in the 1970s. The Ely Hospital Enquiry (1969) gave enormous new drive to what has now become a movement, disturbing the public conscience, forcing governments to think afresh about statutory services, attracting the attention of the media, and giving new hope to mentally handicapped people and their families. The National Society for Mentally Handicapped Children and Adults and the Campaign for Mentally Handicapped People have been highly effective in ensuring that those most directly concerned learned about new developments, and had a concerted strategy for getting them introduced into practice. Finally, the Hester Adrian Centre at Manchester University, the National Development Group (already extinct) and National Development Team, the Warnock and Jay Reports have all been dramatic evidence that a revolution is in progress. It is still too early to say whether it will achieve all of its aims, or where it will end. It is not a British movement, but an international one, with many of its most significant developments happening abroad — in Scandinavia, the USA, or Canada — but the confluence of these streams in British territory has produced an exciting climate for those who are working with mentally handicapped people today.

Where is social work in all this? Sadly, one must say that it has been very much on the sidelines — cheering, maybe, but more often a spectator than a player. By this I do not mean that no exciting things are happening in adult training centres, group homes, hostels and even offices. The freshening breeze has cleared the air for those who work in social services departments as it has for others. They have welcomed the new initiatives, seen applications for their own services and transmitted the ideas to others; but at best have gone on doing familiar things slightly better.

The reasons for this are manifold. The Seebohm reorganisation of 1971, the local government reorganisation of 1973–4, and the health service reorganisation of 1974 have constantly shaken the kaleidoscope for social workers during this period of upheaval. This has led to the loss of specialised knowledge from the former mental health departments (it is generally accepted that the mentally handicapped lost out more than other groups in the reshuffles, because they generate fewer crises). It has meant that social workers are always at full stretch learning new roles or establishing new relationships. It has meant loss of continuity of experience. These are far more destructive processes than we allow ourselves to recognise. And yet they are not an adequate explanation for the reticence of social work. In this period of change only three books have been published in Britain about social work and mental handicap. One — Freda Todd's *Social Work with the Mentally Subnormal* — was written in 1967, before the ferment had properly begun. Another, *The Mentally Subnormal — Social Work Approaches* (1972) edited by Margaret Adams and Howard Lovejoy, was a revision of a book originally published in 1960, and contains little of the excitement of the new wave. The most recent — Christopher Hanvey's *Social Work with Mentally Handicapped People* (1981) — is a useful brief account of the structure of services, rather than a discussion of social work itself. Although books are only a small indicator of practical activity, when new ideas are circulating fast there is a need for practice to absorb them, and the lack of adequate written material is a serious handicap.

This book is a contribution to filling that gap. Its size

precludes a complete survey of the field and fortunately books are readily available about most of the main growth areas. The bibliography suggests a list for further reading, and any social worker who takes his or her role seriously with the mentally handicapped must absorb some of these. Peter Mittler's *People not Patients: Problems and Policies in Mental Handicap* (1979) is an excellent review of current knowledge. Wolf Wolfensberger's *Normalization* (1972) is a key text for understanding the new social approaches to mental handicap.

It is also important to tune oneself in with colleagues, like doctors, teachers and psychologists, by reading some of their texts. Above all it is vital to grasp what parents and mentally handicapped people themselves are saying about their past, their present and their future. These voices come clearly through the publications of the Campaign for Mentally Handicapped People and through *Parents' Voice*. They should be automatically available for any social worker in this field who wants to be up to date.

He or she should also be in touch with the various organisations which have a concern for mentally handicapped people An extensive list of these has been deposited with the library of the National Institute for Social Work in London.
Most of these are a resource for parents as well as professionals, and it should be an aim of social workers to get the list into the hands of every parent of a mentally handicapped person: they need to know where to turn for independent advice and will often need to check even the best professional counsel. They in the end have the decisions to make, and the professionals should see themselves as contributors to parental discussion or to the decisions of mentally handicapped people themselves, not as arbiters on behalf of society.

This book, then, has a limited and specific function. It is about social work practice — the part social workers can or do play in helping mentally handicapped people and their families. In this sense practice can never be perfect. It is always performed in a context which contains both good and bad — a context of old-fashioned policies and older buildings, of colleagues whose personalities are immature, of one's own inadequacies, of government cuts, bureaucratic trivia, cars that will not start and waves of pessimism. I hope to keep these obstacles in mind while considering the bright prospects which have been opened up recently; and while asking what exactly social workers should be doing in the 1980s.

The structure of this book is simple. Like circles on the water its chapters take the attention outwards from the mentally handicapped person to those immediately around him or her: to people encircling the family, to people involved at a distance, and to ordinary functions of society. Anomalies — misfittings — crop up in each wider circle. The question at the back of my mind through it all has been: what kind of role can the social worker properly play here, and how should it be played? The book is designed to help social workers with their problems and not, primarily, to help the mentally handicapped or their parents. But I hope some parents will read it and let me know if it makes sense to them. If it helps them to make sense of their social workers, so much the better. The social workers I have specially in mind are not those who come upon occasional families for whom mental handicap is a problem, but those who have already decided that they want to specialise in work with mentally handicapped people — to confront this particular set of norms and anomalies — and want to think a bit more clearly about them.

Social workers operate in very different settings, and therefore develop quite different approaches to their work. There are many variations, and some jobs are designed to provide a bridge between two settings; but three descriptions will at least suggest the main forms that specialist social work with mentally handicapped people can take. I have chosen a hospital social worker, a social worker employed by a local parents' group, and a social worker based in an area team of the SSD who has the job of establishing and supporting group homes. I am particularly conscious that this list does not recognise the special field of residential social work with mentally handicapped people. In the aftermath of the Jay Report, this area of work requires a book to itself and more detailed coverage than this one can offer.

*   *   *

The first social worker, Sarah, works in a hospital for mentally handicapped people and is employed by the county council. Her field of concern is the 290 patients who live in the hospital and any other family with a mentally handicapped member who chooses to seek help from the hospital staff. In practice, the bulk of her work is in the community outside the hospital. This is because most patients in hospital are very severely handicapped, have been admitted to hospital more or less permanently and have the full-time attention of the nursing staff, whereas people outside may have no help at all unless they are very insistent. The temptation is to leave the in-patients to the care of the nurses, though Sarah would not agree that they have no social work needs, and would prefer to be regularly involved in their reassessment to ensure that their links with the outside world are not forgotten, and that other needs of their families are also borne in mind.

Outside, however, the pressure is very great. There is a large group of families, whose handicapped member was identified many years ago but who have continuing problems, and indeed changing problems, as children grow older or as parents become less able, or the family structure changes in other ways. There is also the trickle of new cases — usually families in a considerable state of crisis as they adjust to the new fact of having a handicapped baby. This second group of families has the more obvious need. When a referral comes in it is usually critical. But such families are usually involved with other professional people: doctors who have delivered the child or make the diagnosis; psychologists who have been testing him or her; or (less often) teachers who have found the child did not fit into a nursery class or primary school. The referral channel is fed by many tributaries and some of these delay the crisis — see the family through the first phase of adjustment, and then pass them on. Meanwhile families with a longstanding problem may suddenly find themselves in an unforeseen crisis: the mother dies, the marriage breaks up, or a tense and unhappy forbearance suddenly breaks down.

Hospitals tend to be under great pressure to admit patients and it is hard to keep beds empty for such emergencies. Therefore, Sarah is valued by the hospital for her ability to keep patients out in the community, and to prevent crises from happening which can disrupt the smooth running of the wards. She has some trouble distinguishing her role from that of the two community nurses employed by the hospital, but they rarely stay long enough to become well known in the community. Sarah is expected to handle criticisms of the hospital by parents of in-patients. On occasion, when she has supported the parents' comments, she has incurred the anger of the nursing staff which has left a residue of mild tension.

She is mostly involved with patients from one geographical area with a population of some 30,000, but because of her special interest in children she also attends the out-patient assessment clinic for children, where she may see patients from other areas.

*   *   *

Caroline works as the welfare officer for a group of parents of mentally handicapped people, organised as a branch of the NSMHC. She is directly employed by them on a part-time basis, and takes her orders, as it were, from their executive committee. In practice she reports to a welfare committee about once a month and this group decides with her what her priorities should be. She responds to requests for help, sometimes coming directly from people in need, sometimes indirectly, through another member of the group or a professional colleague. When she has done a number of visits — twenty or so — she draws together the main themes which have arisen in the course of her contacts and presents these to the welfare group as a subject for discussion. Together they explore the material to see whether there are any indications for action, to try and prevent similar problems arising again. This sort of discussion has given rise to pressure for a support group for parents of a newly identified handicapped baby, for integrated schooling, and for the publication of a booklet for parents about local services.

She does not see her role as a casework one. If she finds that a family has a need for longer-term counselling than she can offer on her occasional visits, she tries to ensure that they find their way to a doctor, social worker or support group, who can provide what they need. She sees herself more as a catalyst, helping people to help themselves, collating information which is not readily available and identifying areas of need which should be tackled at a policy level. This is a more familiar role for community workers than caseworkers and encompasses several areas which conventional social work neglects. In particular it is rooted firmly in consultation with the consumer; it does not get blinded by the details of the individual case, but draws out generalities and sheds work by passing on skills to people who have more time to practise them; it is concerned to represent the consumer to other practitioners and to the authorities, and aims to advise the consumer on professional matters and on tactics for dealing with the authorities. At times this puts Caroline on a collision course with other professionals because her job is given its direction by the consumers. But she is also conscious of her own professional responsibility to advise parents, and at times her advice has not been accepted by them. She is not responsible for managing services other than her own time, nor for explaining the policies of a large organisation.

*   *   *

Bob is responsible for setting up group homes and for supporting their residents. The job was created from 'joint finance' to contribute to the needs of the health service, but he is employed by the county council and based in one divisional team. He covers a wider area than his team, however, with a population of over 200,000. In the last three years he has set up five houses and flats, and sixteen people now live in them. Twelve came from hospital and the other four from their families. Referrals come from hospital staff, from social workers and directly from a few families; and before each house is established he spends a good deal of time assessing prospective residents, helping the group to get to know one another, and planning an individual training programme for each of those who are selected. At first his work was largely centred on finding houses, mostly through the local authority and housing associations, and on organising training programmes, but the support of established residents is now the major component.

He works directly with people who are mentally handicapped, in a way in which other field social workers do not, and is very conscious of their being stigmatised and patronised even by those who wish to help them. This is particularly true of the early stages in each household, when former carers − parents or nurses − tend to intervene much too readily and make it hard for residents to solve their own problems. At the beginning he had to deal with a good deal of suspicion and anxiety from parents especially, but this has now modulated into cautious benevolence as the houses have produced few crises. There are problems every month in the relationships within the houses, or in practical matters, and it is clear that continuing support will be needed for the foreseeable future. There is therefore a growing workload which is making it harder to establish new houses. This is causing tension with Bob's seniors who are anxious to keep the project moving. Bob feels he has a primary responsibility, however, to those who are already out on their own.

*   *   *

These three jobs are radically different from one another, in lines of accountability, systems of support, relationships with colleagues and choice of clients. The three people could easily be working in the same geographical area, with minimal contact with one another. They might even feel competitive with one another, or disagree with one another's philosophy and method of working. Yet they are all qualified social workers, appropriately employed. There is legitimate conflict of interest between parents and children, suppliers and consumers of service, statutory and voluntary providers: there has to be room for debate about priorities. But there must also be a way of resolving these differences inherent in structure, and other differences of a more personal kind, so that the common tasks of bringing services to the needy, understanding individual situations, or creating new services can be performed most effectively. Because social workers approach these tasks from different directions it sometimes seems hard to identify the common elements in their work. As I have suggested earlier, this is because their function for society is to deal with people who are being left out of other systems, of the ordinary range of services. There is no reason why Bob's job should not be done through a programme organised by the housing and education departments; but most schools do not take preparation for independent living seriously enough and do not continue it long enough, and most housing welfare officers do not at present take seriously the job of helping groups of unrelated people to live together. Until a combined programme like this is devised, there will be a need for someone like a group homes officer to help one group of marginal people. There is a similar need for parents to have their own service, so long as statutory services do not work closely enough with them, and do not represent their views as consumers strongly enough. And hospitals always deal with certain groups at the expense of others. Social workers who fight for one marginal group naturally become identified with them, at the expense of others. This is what they are paid to do and one cannot quarrel with them for doing it. One must, however, ask whether in their diversity there are not also common causes which may get lost. Creating a structure which allows them to meet and find those common causes is clearly of great importance. Only then is it likely that social workers could take an effective lead in the field of mental handicap.

The rest of the book will be concerned with common causes; but it will be clear at many points that the perspectives of social workers in different jobs will vary, and that they will choose different ways of approaching the same problems. I hope it will be possible for readers to make their own applications of the general points that are made.

The examples given in the text are based on social workers' experience, but are fictionalised to prevent embarrassment to individuals.

1

The Concept of Social Work and the Concept of Handicap

This is a book about practice, not a treatise about philosophy; but it cannot start without some discussion about attitudes and assumptions. The title brings together two terms – 'social work' and 'mental handicap' – which are wide and woolly, not only in common parlance but in the language of experts. It will not be good enough to plunge in without showing what I mean by them.

Social work

Social work is the less satisfactory of the two. It can be found in use to describe the middle class running jumble sales, nosey neighbours checking up on one another, vicars calming the bereaved, scoutmasters taking awkward boys up mountains. In a more professional sense it is used of home help organisers, health visitors, occupational therapists, psychiatric nurses doing home visits, GPs talking about money problems. Fair enough. These are all social, and they are all work. But are they what social workers mean when they use the term?

There is a now-notorious definition of social work – a definition by social workers – which says it is 'applied love'. Is every lover a social worker? There is another, which says it is:

The purposeful and ethical application of personal skills in inter-personal relationships directed towards enhancing the personal and social functioning of an individual, family, group or neighbourhood, which necessarily involves using evidence obtained from practice to help create a social environment conducive to the well-being of all (BASW, 1977, p. 19).

Ho hum! Many a high-class brothel-keeper could accept that model, if she could make sense of it.

We all make our own statements about these things. I want to isolate one factor, which I believe to be crucial and not very well understood. Social workers deal with people who are in conflict with some norm of the society in which they live; they may be in conflict with many. Sometimes they are not aware that they are in conflict; sometimes they have set out to create the conflict. The essence of the social work task is the resolution of that conflict. There are many kinds of resolution, and many means to reach resolution; so social workers are seen to be doing many different kinds of work. But if the conflict of norms is not present, then they are not doing social work even if they are working socially.

Norms come in all shapes and sizes. They are ways of seeing and doing things. As children we learn to organise our perceptions in certain ways — taught by parents and peers, teachers, legislators and broadcasters. We learn to suppress visions that are 'silly' or 'childish' or otherwise unacceptable, and to use polarising mental glasses. In the end we can only see things in certain ways, unless we are poets, or just waking up, or high on something. Acceptable ways of seeing things are norms and people who insist on seeing differently are often in trouble.

Similarly, we learn to *act* in acceptable ways: to drive on the correct side of the road, eat with our mouths shut, not uproot flowers, help old ladies across roads, not laugh at cripples, speak in intelligible sentences. Some people cannot or will not do things in the normal way, and they too get into trouble. Some do not know what the rules are: children, strangers, those who have lost their memory. Some know the rules, but cannot work to them: the handicapped, the sick, people under great stress of feeling. Some actively want to break the rules: adolescents looking for their own identity, people who have not had their needs met within the rules, reformers. These people are not very unusual. We all of us have been in these categories at one time or another and will be again, many times, before we die. So there are more rules for dealing with people who break rules, and social systems — schools, courts and prisons, isolation wards, madhouses, carnivals, celebrations and so on — to encompass rule-breaking and rule-breakers. These hold them in temporary control while letting the main system go on. There are also millions of minor ways in which rule-breakers are tolerated and kept in line. Neighbours nudge one another back into place; they help one another to act normally; they disguise one another's eccentricity, at least from outsiders; they check out their normality with one another. Mostly this works. When it does not, the social worker is called in. That is my point of departure.

There is an area of ambiguity where no one knows if it is a job for the social worker or not. Have neighbours really tried what they can do? Are the forces that work against normal behaviour unusually strong, or have neighbours just drawn back? The more social workers will take on, the more they will be left to do. So sometimes social workers can be seen doing perfectly ordinary tasks where there is no real conflict of norms. I prefer not to call this social work and will be using the term more narrowly in this book.

Social workers are concerned about conflict of norms. However, they are concerned not just to fit individuals to the norm — to keep the rules obeyed — but also to rethink the rules. Often rules do not fit individuals. Some people suffer because they are living inside a system that ignores them or makes impossible demands on them. If they are to survive, they may have to break the rules. Social workers must be expected to see this; they must be expected to challenge the rules; and sometimes they must be understood if they help people to break them. They cannot claim immunity from the rules of course, and must explain what they are at, but it is part of the essence of the job to operate in the no-man's-land between the norms and the people outside them.

Whether it is possible for social workers to maintain this position when they are nearly all employed by local government is a moot and lively point. Local government exists to represent the majority view — the norm. Can it really handle the conflict of employing people who are prepared to be critical of the norm? One of the ways in which it has handled this conflict recently is to camouflage the norm-critique under flurries of other activity: service delivery, for example, getting bath aids to the handicapped or old people to day centres. The public understands such activities; it is comfortable for social workers to say, 'See how kind and helpful we are'. If they came out into the open and said, 'We are here for the misfits', the funds would fade away. But they *are* there for misfits, in the sense of people whom others disapprove of, or just do not want to know.

Mental handicap

What about mental handicap? Handicap relates to a norm. Physical handicap relates to the norm of the human body; mental handicap to the norm of the human mind. But those norms are not fixed and immutable: they are products of current taste. In one generation bosoms are in and bottoms are out; in the next the reverse is true. If the ideal male is six feet tall, weighs 160 pounds and has a prominent chin, then small weedy men or large fat men are handicapped. Of course some norms persist. The idea that humans should have two legs, two arms and eyes in front of the head has persisted for a very long time. Tails have been out for almost as long. But in our changing world it does not take very much imagination to picture a world in which legs become a handicap. We colonise another planet which has minimal gravity and mobility is achieved by flapping the hands in the air. Then excessive limbs become a problem and tiny hands are useless. How long will it take natural selection to catch up with the move? Some of our wheelchair occupants will be released – will indeed be the athletes of the new world.

Fanciful, but the point is clear. Science fiction relies upon it. We are not dealing with absolutes. To make the point in a different way, think what would happen if Neanderthal Man reappeared in Europe. He would instantly be registrable as physically handicapped, supposing he were not classified as an ape. But in his time he may have been the top of the tree. He lost out in the end because some other kind of hominoid had a bigger brain. Probably the ones with the bigger brains looked monstrous at first, were avoided by potential mates and had a struggle to survive. The world did not fit them very well. But now they (we) have organised the world to suit us.

Handicap is something relative, determined by the circumstances of a particular time and place; something socially defined. We could remove it by redefining the world, just as we can remove mobility handicaps by removing steps. The world is designed to suit the majority whose muscles and brains work in a particular way. But who says they *should* work like that? It seems to be convenient − it has proven survival value − but there is no moral imperative here. We have a norm, and against it some people measure up badly. Does that mean that we have to look at them as distorted and unwhole? When you look at a mentally handicapped child, what do you see? Be honest. A vegetable? An animal? A sad travesty of God's own image? Unless you have experienced these feelings, you are not going to be able to work with the mentally handicapped; or at least you are not going to be able to work with the people associated with them. Of course you have to see the child, the whole human being, the potential lover, the helper of others. But if you do not take the weight of the clash with the norm, you do not really know what the problem is.

Mentally handicapped people, their families and other supporters need plenty of help. Much of it can come from ordinary reactions of friends and neighbours, from information sheets and straight advice. None of that is social work, in my terms. Social work involves sorting out the conflict of norms, when it is too great to handle in a particular situation. That may occur because no one has had to think about the problem before, someone is frightened by the clash of contexts, or other pressures make it hard to think straight.

We should make sure that where there is a conflict of norms which is not being resolved, social workers are available to help. We should also make sure that information and advice are available to everyone who needs to know about mental handicap. We should not confuse these two issues, even though there are advantages in confusing them. More people need information than need social work, so it is easier to get money for the former. Some people will see social work as an admission of failure and will find it easier to ask for information in the first place. Finally, admitting that conflict of norms is possible makes it harder for society at large to slip out of the arena. If the problem can be seen as technical — to be dealt with by experts — then there is nothing for the rest of us to do; and if, after receiving information and advice, someone still has a problem, it is a personal problem, to be dealt with by therapeutic means.

But it is not only a personal problem: it is a problem also in the way that society encompasses anomaly. It is not just a matter of mentally handicapped people fitting in, but of the rest of us fitting out. To borrow Paul Williams's title, we have a 'mutual handicap' (Williams, 1978).

There is a further point. Much of the social work done with mentally handicapped people and their families is not in fact about mental handicap but often about other family problems: marital discord, disturbed children, poor educational performance, unemployment, poor housing and rent arrears, illness, depression, old age, bereavement, crime, aggression. The mentally handicapped person may play a part in these things, but it is not to be *assumed* that they exist because there is a mentally handicapped person around.

The role of social work

I have suggested that social work is concerned with anomaly — with those people whose needs are not met by the established social structure or who are indeed damaged by it. People have many kinds of need and social structures are usually designed to meet one kind of need, although they sometimes have to meet others secondarily. Health services are designed to maintain the integrity of the human body, though they may have to provide food and shelter as means to that end. Education structures are designed to transfer skills from generation to generation, to train labour and to help individuals to create, but to achieve this they must provide buildings and heating and sometimes food. Social work is peculiar in that it concerns itself with needs of every kind: for example, food, shelter, health care, education. It does so, not for the whole population in need, but for a few people whose needs would not otherwise be met; and not as the holder of some special expertise in each area of need, but improvising, to fill gaps as best may be, borrowing other people's knowledge where possible.

Why is it that some people do not have their needs adequately met by the normal services which are designed to meet them. There are six main reasons. First, some people do not know that the normal services exist or believe that they are not eligible for them. Second, some people either have not learned common social skills or scorn to use them in situations where they feel at a disadvantage and thereby disqualify themselves from service: for example, inability to fill in forms or read instructions, to control one's anger at inefficiency or insensitivity, or to keep appointments. Third, some people live eccentric lives, or have secrets they are unwilling to reveal, or otherwise do not accord with expectations about how people should behave: they may therefore meet incomprehension when they turn to services for help. Fourth, some people have significant needs in more than one area of their lives at the same time and are thereby prevented from using services which are designed for one need alone: for example, the old who are also blind, or social security applicants who are also homeless. Fifth, there are people for whom the means of meeting their need have not yet been devised: some technical or imaginative break-through is needed. Finally, there are people who are waiting for a new discovery to reach them, through the impasses of incomprehension or lack of resources which are usual for a time.

It is small wonder that the caseloads of social workers are such a miscellany; nor that attempts to describe what social workers do, or why they do it, are so unsatisfactory. Social workers deal with exceptions and misfits — marginal people who have been defined out of someone else's system. It is no more to be expected that they will all fit in to a single social service structure than that whales and lizards will fit a common category merely because the one is not a fish and the other is not a mammal.

What should social workers do?

From the categories of people just described, it follows that social workers will have to perform a variety of tasks. They will have to:

1. Put people in touch with existing services.
2. Negotiate for people or teach social skills.
3. Be open-minded themselves and have a personal enough relationship with people to understand the meaning of unconventional behaviour, and to convey that understanding to others.
4. Arrange for services to be extended or for new services to be provided to cover multiple need.
5. Attempt to find solutions or encourage others to find solutions to unsolved problems.
6. Publicise and campaign for the adoption of new solutions which have been found.

Some of these tasks are not necessarily social work ones. Putting people in touch with existing services, for instance, could be the job of an information service and of those who first encounter the unmet need. Likewise where new ways of helping are known to exist but are not yet provided, it could be the job of the needy and their immediate supporters to campaign for implementation. These are the 'normalising' ways of meeting the need. They restore the needy to the ranks of ordinary citizens and do not insist on a category for whales and lizards. Social workers have made efforts to suggest that they provide a 'normal' service for the whole population, but this is clearly not how they are seen; nor, if my analysis is correct, should it be so. They can, however, try to ensure that whenever possible solutions are provided by 'normal' services and convey clearly that their own first priority must lie with the abnormal and unconventional. The specialist subject matter of social work will then be seen to be social structure and social anomaly, and the status of individual people in that context.

How does this bear on mental handicap?

The foregoing analysis suggests that there are three main

activities for social workers with mentally handicapped people. First, to make sure people are getting what is available. Second, to get to know them well enough to make a personal response to their special needs. Third, to work out a strategy for making new services available and to do all of these things in alliance with anyone else who is interested to help, especially mentally handicapped people themselves and their families. The present situation requires all three of these elements.

Most of the book will be about the second element, since it is the one in which social work has something special to offer. But there is no question that the first is essential. Most of the criticisms of social workers by parents of mentally handicapped people are of impracticality and failure to organise effective relief on a practical plane. It need not be the social worker's job to do this, but unless it is done, parents will be right to feel aggrieved and will be unable to consider other matters. Any social worker who wants to be taken seriously will ensure that information is made available to parents about the nature of mental handicap, the problems of daily living, existing local services and about good ideas from elsewhere.

Making sure people get what is available

It seems astonishing in a society which is increasingly obsessed with data collection and the transmission of information that many people can remain ignorant of what exists on their doorstep, or of their eligibility for help. It is clear that this is true, however. The Chronically Sick and Disabled Persons Act (1970) laid a duty on local authorities to ensure that they know of anyone in their area who is disabled, mentally or physically. Few authorities have taken this duty seriously and some have defended their inaction on the grounds that it is unfair to stir up expectations of help when little exists. This form of rationing by ignorance always places the least able at a disadvantage and must be viewed as discriminatory practice. It is essential, therefore, as a first step, to create a register of the mentally handicapped.

In theory this should not be difficult for children, because the health visitor is statutorily involved with all children from birth; and all children are monitored by the school medical service throughout their primary and secondary education. There are a number of problems, however, as Atkinson (1981) pointed out. Some children are not diagnosed early, but are gradually found to be in educational difficulty, which is not properly recorded. Some children move from one area to another, without information being transferred from one register to another. Some service personnel, nurses or doctors, social workers, psychologists and teachers, may be unaware that a register exists, or do not record facts that are known to them. Finally there may be objections, on the grounds of confidentiality, to the recording of information, obtained in one context and for one purpose, in a register held in another place for unspecified purposes. A GP, for instance, who is involved in a difficult process of trying to help parents to accept that their child is mentally handicapped, may be rightly anxious that if the child's name is placed on a register someone will talk or write to the parents without due sensitivity to their feelings. Or a social worker may learn from parents who have just moved to the area that they do not wish to have anything to do with the health services in view of past difficulties. Clearly there must be room for these exclusions, temporarily or permanently, but this should not be allowed to prevent the creation of a register for others.

With adults it may be even harder to establish an effective register. Even if past school records are available it may be hard to trace adults who have moved. Some of the older ones may never have been in the education system. Some people who may be classed as mentally handicapped have been brain-damaged as adults by illness or accident, and this group may not be easy to find. And some mentally handicapped people may be living successful independent lives and would not wish to be included on a register.

The pros and cons of establishing registers of this kind have now been reviewed many times. In many areas there still seems to be doubt about their value, however, and it is worth reviewing what has already been said by researchers before going into battle on this issue. The key reference is the study by Jones (1979). (Other reviews have been made by Stephen

Mitchell of Hounslow Social Services Department Civic Centre, Lampton Road, Hounslow, London TW3 4DN, and by Lambeth Social Services Department Research Section, Blue Star House, 234/244 Stockwell Road, London SW9 9SR.)

A register is only valuable if it is used to ensure that those who are on it are given information and access to new services, and to find out what needs they have. If this is its purpose, it is likely to be acceptable to most people. However it pre-supposes that there is a system for collecting and publishing relevant information. Some information will be supplied by individual services at particular times, but a great deal of valuable information is tucked away in services which are not good at publicity. Many local societies for mentally handi-capped children have therefore attempted to collate facts and suggestions from their members and from local professionals. This goes a long way to guarantee that the contents will be practical, and is often preferable to social workers and others trying to do the job themselves. The guides by the Bristol, Cambridge, Cardiff or South Glamorgan societies are good examples; and as the process of compilation necessarily involves a good deal of exchange and discussion, both among parents about what should be included, and between parents and professionals, it is a valuable way to provoke a higher level of collaboration. If no one else seems to have taken the initiative to produce a guide, it can be very valuable for a social worker to call together a meeting of those likely to be interested. The problems of production and financing are significant, but in a group of people from a variety of agencies and backgrounds they tend to resolve themselves in ways no one could have predicted beforehand.

Sensitive provision of information goes a long way beyond mailing lists and guides, however. The difficult problem of parents who have not yet accepted that their child is mentally handicapped has already been mentioned. This illustrates the general point that information must be supplied at the right time and in the right way. There are a number of predictable periods when parents need information: the crucial one is at the moment of diagnosis, but going to school and leaving it are also important crises. Other times may be less predictable: when parents want to consider short-term residential care;

when the problem of sexual maturation starts to worry them; if they need reassurance that their child will be looked after when they have gone; and if they are wanting to consider types of more independent living. Individual parents will have a need for specific information about their own situation, and it is an obvious preliminary to good social work to have knowledge of the range of books, pamphlets and journals which are currently available about mental handicap in general, about particular conditions, educational problems or ways of helping. Again it is not the social worker's job to give detailed information about medical or educational matters. If, however — and the situation is not uncommon — the social worker discovers that the information systems of other services are less than satisfactory, it is important to try to get this altered. Sometimes this can be done directly through a colleague in the other service; but sometimes it may be necessary to work together with the local parents' group or other professionals to demonstrate that the need really exists, before the relevant service will take notice.

Even when people have been given information they may not readily digest it. The problem with comprehensive guides which contain a large amount of information, is that the two or three points which might be relevant to a particular family may be hidden among the rest. And some families are unable to cope with written matter at all. But a reference guide has the great advantage that it can be taken in over a long period and consulted when specific problems have arisen, and should be cross-referenced with this in mind. It cannot, however, entirely remove the need for opportunities to have questions answered face to face.

Ensuring that people get the services which exist is also not just a matter of information. It may be necessary to encourage some parents to test their eligibility. It may also be necessary to press service-providers to do their duty. The value of a good local parents' group as a pressure group of those directly concerned, and as a source of information about how services actually work in practice, is enormous. This may be particularly true if the pressure has to be applied to the SSD or to the hospital in which a social worker works. It is all too easy for social workers to fall out with parents' groups, when they are being critical of the SSD, and social workers identify themselves too closely with the local authority. The social worker's first responsibility is to his or her clients: to learn their needs and make sure that they are represented as strongly as possible to planners and policy-makers. This professional concern cannot be overridden by the separate responsibility to an employer, although there may be times when it is necessary to explain to a client why particular decisions have been made, and even to say to them that they are overstating their case or are wrong in some respect. Often, however, this kind of tension can be kept to a minimum if the people involved are known to one another. A useful event for keeping lines of communication open, and in particular for drawing in new parents of a mentally handicapped child, is an annual day conference at which the various services are invited to set out their stall and describe their work. A series of evening meetings might achieve the same end, but may be harder for parents to attend.

Some of the families who are most in need are the least likely to attend meetings: those who have several young children, who are isolated in their own community and therefore cannot find baby-sitters, who have only one parent, who are depressed or hostile to authority, who live in isolated areas and have no means of transport or cannot afford bus fares. Making sure that these families get to know that services exist and how to make contact with them very often requires a visiting service. People who are in such situations should be identified on the register and should have priority for contact at home. Some local parents' societies ensure that this happens by organising a panel of visitors for their members and for new families referred to them, and this is probably the ideal way for contact to be maintained with the majority. But it is important to keep in mind the families for whom common sense is not enough. Parents who do not fit in with ordinary social conventions – those who are abrupt, for instance, or give no return for help offered – are no more popular with the parents of mentally handicapped people than with anyone else. It is therefore important for social workers, whose job it is to deal with the misfitting, to have an independent view of who is being visited and who is not.

Of the various ideas that have been mooted for ensuring that such contact is maintained, the concept of a key worker is probably the most effective. For everyone on the register, one contact should be nominated. This could be a doctor or community nurse, a social worker, occupational therapist, teacher or another parent. He or she would be chosen in conjunction with the family and everyone involved would know who had been nominated. His or her responsibility would be to keep contact with the family, to alert appropriate services if help is needed and to be the fail-safe point of contact. This in no way implies that other services would withdraw: they would continue to perform their ordinary functions, and the family would be free to contact them directly; but in the event of contact failing for any reason, the key worker would be available to re-establish it.

Like many good ideas the key worker hangs or falls by the degree of co-operation already achieved in a particular area. Where the services are working together comfortably, there will probably be opportunities to meet and agree on the nomination of key workers. Where this does not happen, the choice of key workers may cause some difficulty. It may seem to imply that one service is more acceptable than another; or alternatively that one service is willing to undertake more routine work than another. Some people may feel that the key worker will intrude on the functions of other services or that the whole scheme will be a bureaucratic waste of time. These are all alarm bells that collaboration is not as good as it should be, and should direct attention to the machinery for co-operation.

Finally, one must give some thought to the unconscious messages that services give to their clients. When resources are in short supply — which is the usual situation — there are strong incentives for service personnel to remain silent, while not actively discouraging applicants for help. Often this happens unintentionally. A doctor or social worker mentally reviews what can *practically* be done to help a client and simply rules out services which are hard to obtain. The client never hears of them, therefore, and is not in a position to make the request which might lead to an improvement, nor to organise the protest or the lobby which might produce political action. This kind of fudging, done with the best of intentions, is what makes it so hard to identify gaps in service. Ideally there should be a prescription in each case of what the client really needs as well as what can actually be obtained. The difference should be monitored and the needs should then be built into the next round of service planning. Sometimes, indeed, the silence of service personnel seems to imply that no solutions exist. There is a world of difference between believing that no one ever gets a child into short-term care — that it does not exist — and believing that one's local services are inadequate and perhaps uncaring. It may make no difference in terms of getting a placement, but it provides a target for parents' anger and political action which is a far healthier situation from their point of view.

Using the register as a way of discovering need involves other mechanisms besides those of information provision. The Campaign for Mentally Handicapped People has suggested (Newsletter 3) that social services departments should be responsible for assessing everyone on the register, as to their capacity for community living, visiting every six months and reviewing the needs and abilities of clients annually. If this were done seriously, in the manner of the Individual Programme Planning (IPP) scheme described in chapter 6, it would be an extremely effective way of identifying need and of providing the evidence needed to renew services. Most SSDs do not begin to move in this direction. They are too busy with 'statutory' work, do not have the resources, and so on. But there are resources, in the staff already committed to work with mentally handicapped people, in hospitals, hostels, adult training centres and the community at large. There are further resources in local associations and in schools, which could also be mobilised. Not everyone on the register needs to see a social worker: what they need is to see someone who has a clear responsibility to ask a few key questions about their needs and wishes, and to report back.

The question of planning and taking political action to introduce new services will be resumed in chapter 6. The next four chapters are about the second element of the social worker's role — personal communication with the individual people involved in the care and education of mentally handicapped people, including of course themselves.

2

Relating to Mentally Handicapped People

Until 1886 mentally handicapped people were officially classified with lunatics. If their families could not look after them they were sent to county asylums, poor-houses or prison. Many were shut away in back rooms of their homes, farmed out as cheap labour or otherwise maltreated. Perhaps some were amiably accepted as the 'village idiot' of our mythology. At the end of the century they were cast as the villains of eugenic melodrama, breeding faster than the rest of the population and polluting the national bloodstream. To control this supposed epidemic, voluntary organisations sprang up to supervise the 'feeble-minded' in their own homes: segregation for life was seen as an enlightened aim for them and special education was begun. In the 1913 Mental Deficiency Act three grades were defined: idiot, imbecile and feeble-minded, together with the notorious category of 'moral defective'. Local voluntary organisations grew helter-skelter to see the 1913 Act implemented and undertook many statutory functions for local authorities, such as ascertainment. They were the basis of the voluntary movement in mental health as we know it. We still live in the traditions of that period. Although there is no longer the same anxiety about eugenics, mentally handicapped people are still treated as if they were a burden and a danger, and it is often felt to be shameful for parents to have a child who is mentally handicapped. Although the dangers of institutionalisation are well documented, a huge number of mentally handicapped people still live in large hospitals from which only a few get out. And society expects parents to look after their mentally handicapped children but is clearly reluctant to pay much attention to their needs when they do so.

Nevertheless attitudes are changing. For ten years it has been established beyond any doubt that even the most severely mentally handicapped people can learn far more than was thought possible. Mentally handicapped people have whole personalities and can relate to others as warm and sensitive human beings. All they need to make a contribution to society is receptiveness on the part of society. Since they now live in a society which is unreceptive to the contribution of many non-handicapped people, this cannot be taken for granted. Over the same period many of the new structures that are needed to make this revolution have been invented, described, retried, prefabricated and advertised. The institutions could go if we could free ourselves of the past and its values. But norms change very slowly. Like Huntington's Chorea, they are transferred to the next generation before it is realised that they exist; so it will be many years before the eugenic fears and the belief in segregation have died away. Perhaps they never will. Segregation, after all, is a classic way of dealing with anomalous people of all types and is the usual first reaction of any society to its deviant members.

Who are the mentally handicapped?

Mental handicap is traditionally defined in either medical or psychological terms. The medical definition restricts the term (or its surrogates, like mental deficiency, mental subnormality or mental retardation) to people who can be identified by some verifiable damage to their bodies or some failure to develop in recognisable physical ways. The psychologists attempt to restrict it to people whose performance in intelligence or other tests does not reach the level characteristic of their age group. There is also a third line of thought which allows its use for people who are unable to achieve conventional levels of performance in ordinary everyday tasks. Theoretically there are difficulties with all these kinds of definition and they do not always coincide conveniently. For instance, some people with clear-cut medical conditions, like Down's Syndrome, show levels of ability close to the normal range and may be able to perform common tasks with great proficiency. On the other hand, many people who show no evidence of damage or underdevelopment may be unable to do well in tests, and many highly intelligent people are incompetent in daily tasks or in making a success of their lives.

In practice, the term 'mentally handicapped' is used loosely in many situations and the services for mentally handicapped people are offered to some who fit these criteria — and sometimes only one of them — very vaguely. The largest marginal group is of children called mildly educationally subnormal (an offensive term, usually expurgated as ESN/M), among whom can be found many who suffer from emotional problems, are culturally deprived or have simultaneous disadvantages, physical, emotional and cultural. These children, by definition, approach the educational norm, and in some cases can be transferred to ordinary schools. They and their adult equivalents are often neglected by the services for mentally handicapped people within the health and social services and have been largely ignored in the revolution of the last ten years. They and their families represent a clientele who, because of their various and often acute disabilities and deprivations, require the attentions of social workers. The specialist services for mentally handicapped people may not be the best fitted to help them; their needs may be very different from those of the severely educationally subnormal (ESN/S). Most recent developments in thinking about mentally handicapped people have been stimulated by the problems of institutionalisation, which is less often an issue for the ESN/M. This book follows the pattern, by concentrating on the ESN/S, or those who are severely mentally handicapped. Some of the things described will be relevant to the former group also, but this will not necessarily be so. It is important to make this point, not only to clarify what the book is about, but to point out the special needs of the ESN/M. They are in some danger of becoming a neglected group, caught in the boundary area between ordinary education and special education. It is only one of the ironies of their situation that the discussion about normalisation has concentrated on the more severely handicapped group. There is at least a distant possibility that severely handicapped children might be placed in ordinary schools, while the ESN/M are left in their segregation.

They are not the only marginal group who need recognition. In most schools or hospitals or hostels for mentally handicapped people there will be found a small number of children or adults who suffer not from mental handicap but from other conditions: childhood autism, emotional maladjustment, epilepsy, adult psychotic conditions, and not least from institutionalisation. There are others whose condition has not been defined. These people find themselves in the care of services for mentally handicapped people because their social adjustment is poor, their conditions are not well understood, special services have not been designed for them and there is nowhere else for them to go. This is not necessarily a bad thing, but it often turns out to create difficulties which must be understood. They have special needs as well as common ones and the services must be especially sensitive to pick these up. Just as certain apparently dull children in ordinary schools may be found to be partially deaf or to have restricted eyesight, or a disruptive pupil may turn out to be bright and bored, so some of these individual pupils may be masking their real ability in some areas of their lives or, just as important, their real wishes.

*   *   *

Paul is in foster care, after severe rejection in his own family. He is very disturbed and often withdrawn. He is afraid to fail and even hides his achievements. His teacher has to guess what he can really do and move on to new things, without checking, for fear of frightening him. His achievements, if she is lucky, emerge later. He is in fact a depressed little boy, of low average ability, who has adopted a pose like mental handicap as a way of masking his anxiety.

*   *   *

Next, one must recognise that those who are mentally handicapped by any definition may also have other disabilities. Physical handicap is common, but they may also be emotionally disturbed or mentally ill. Some have lived in families under extreme stress; some have been rejected and moved from one setting to another all their lives; some have been subject to cruelty and neglect. These factors need attention quite as much as the mental handicap. In fact the mental handicap may be entirely misleading. It is easy to think that a mentally handicapped person is a problem or that he has a problem, because he is mentally handicapped. That may be true. But he may have, or be, a problem for quite other reasons, which must not be ignored.

Finally one must recognise (it is an allied point) that mentally handicapped people are themselves all individual people: old and young, male and female, vivacious or morose by nature, adventurous or cautious, conservative or (yes) radical, biddable or stubborn. Labels create stereotypes which it is hard to see beyond. One cannot talk without using them, but if one assumes that people with the same label have all things in common one may be hopelessly misled. They have different problems; they also have different resources, hopes and viewpoints. This is true at every level of ability or disability although, as communication becomes more difficult, it may become harder for strangers to perceive the differences.

Mentally handicapped people range from the profoundly handicapped to the nearly normal and it is foolish to seem to suggest that they are all the same. In relating to the profoundly handicapped a social worker needs to use as much sensitivity and imagination as in relating to any frightened child or any depressed adult − that is, sensitivity not to the fear or the depression but to the individual person in whom they are found.

The experience of being mentally handicapped

How can we know what mentally handicapped people are going through? How do we make the imaginative leap from our own experience to theirs? If we are to be sensitive to their needs we have to guess what the world feels like to them and what their reactions mean. There is a trap here: that we need for our own sake to find meaning, and therefore impute it as parents do to tiny babies or owners sometimes do to pets. But unless we really believe the vegetable hypothesis that 'he is only a cabbage', then the experience of mentally handicapped people is organised and has some kind of meaning, however profound the handicap. It is important to stress this point, since one hears, even today, of people – even professionals – who are not convinced that mentally handicapped people have normal sensory experiences. A dentist, for instance, told a mother that he had used an anaesthetic for an extraction 'although these children do not feel pain like other people do'. It is clear that mentally handicapped children make conceptual links, but that they do so more rarely, more slowly. And while other children seem to go looking for links, testing sight against sound or touch against taste, mentally handicapped children are often much more passive, do not experiment to the same degree and therefore have fewer experiences to associate with one another.

An important part of compensatory training, therefore, must be to expand their pool of experience and help them to make links by constant repetition. It is also important to become conscious of the links which are most crucial or nodal. Parents are not used to thinking carefully about the order in which their children acquire links: they happen in such profusion that they could not be monitored and on the whole, the sequence of necessary steps sorts itself out. With mentally handicapped children this may not be so. It may be necessary to find ways of provoking a mentally handicapped child to listen, make noises or merely make spontaneous actions, before it is possible to move to the crucial first word. A good deal of work has been done on these areas of development and social workers should be familiar with works like Mary la Frenais's little booklet, *Language Stimulus and Retarded Children*, (1971) and the checklists in Cunningham and Jeffree, *Working with Parents* (1971). Other useful references will be found in the bibliography.

Some children will never produce a word. This does not mean that they cannot develop as people or have no skills at all. Sometimes the concepts are clearly there, while expression is lacking, as in the case of Joey Deacon (1974), who could only communicate through his friend Ernie, who alone understood his inarticulate sounds. Sometimes it is doubtful even that concepts have been formed, but parents or regular staff can register reactions and identify feelings in small gestures.

Others will come close to the achievements of Nigel Hunt, who had it said of him at the age of 4: 'Oh yes. A little mongoloid. Quite ineducable. Do you want him put away?' By the age of 11 he could write of his pony (typing it himself): 'He always got Cornflakes and how he enjoyed them, and all the suzzle of the nice crispy flakes went all down his mouth and "Eh what a mess" ' (Hunt, 1967). Nigel's poetic talent is by no means unique, though it was nurtured by parents who appreciated language. His and Joey Deacon's books illustrate the fact that mentally handicapped people think very concretely and do not easily generalise from their experience: it is perhaps harder for them to make links between two situations which are similar in some respects but not in others, or to distinguish between situations which are dissimilar but also similar.

The theory of discrimination learning is highly relevant to this fact and it is worth outlining some of its concepts. They are not only valuable in formal training situations but also in establishing new behaviour in domestic situations. Learning a new skill involves several components. It involves the performance itself — taking action of an appropriate kind — but it also involves understanding the task. Sometimes this is very simple ('Open your mouth') but sometimes it is very complex ('Take the green cord in your left hand and put it behind the large post'). Failure to make a correct distinction between green and red, left and right, behind and in front or large and small, will make it impossible to perform the task. Studies have shown that the problem for mentally handicapped people is predominantly in such discriminations rather than in actual performance. Once they have been grasped, mentally handicapped people can learn the actions as quickly as other people and can perform as effectively. It is therefore important to teach the distinctions before trying to put the whole task together.

Establishing new distinctions or discriminations of this kind can sometimes be facilitated by using an established distinction which is later 'faded out'. For instance, to distinguish between left and right, the hands can be associated with an established colour distinction — red and green perhaps — and then, in a gradual series of changes, the colours are faded to a common grey, while the words 'left' and 'right' alone are used as cues. In teaching about coins it may be necessary to establish an easy distinction between very large and very small discs and then to vary the sizes so that subtler distinctions are grasped. 'Easy-to-hard' sequences represent another powerful tool in training.

A key factor in such training is attention, and work done in the early 1960s (Zeaman and House, 1963) demonstrated that this is especially important with mentally handicapped people. Colour and novelty greatly aid attention. Gold and Scott (1971) have given a good account of this. They also suggest that it is important to select a clear criterion of success when training — six consecutive correct solutions, for instance — and work to this. It is then possible to evaluate exactly what has been achieved and when training may cease. It is valuable to train 'beyond criterion' in order to establish the behaviour firmly; and it is vital not to permit the development of 'failure sets' — expectation of failure — by continuing with techniques which are not effective and only produce loss of attention. These last points are of great practical importance for parents and others who work with mentally handicapped people. A great deal of adult behaviour towards mentally handicapped people has been described as 'lukewarm teaching' (Morton, 1979); they hover and assist the learner in a rather unpredictable way, so that it is never quite clear whether he has achieved success or not by his own resources. This is as true of dressing or shopping as of workbench attitudes. Establishing a clear aim makes it possible to evaluate training and learning; and makes it clear to the trainee whether he has succeeded and how far he is independent. 'Lukewarm teaching' is one reason why parents and teachers sometimes overestimate the ability of a learner, and therefore never complete the training task. Making teaching more powerful, Gold argues, is a matter of breaking tasks down into small steps, setting clear goals, and arranging highly structured periods of training which may be quite brief, rather than long periods at complex tasks which are not monitored.

Such teaching is a time-consuming business, but it is clearly efficient in the long run if it makes people better able to do things for themselves. More time is lost by feeding, dressing and accompanying mentally handicapped people who might not need these things done for them, and by ineffective training rituals and assessment which leads nowhere, than would be consumed in effective training. When tasks are adequately broken down, moreover, it becomes possible to use unskilled teachers, like parents or volunteers, for specific training roles.

The mentally handicapped person as a subject

There is one significant danger in this approach to training which otherwise offers such a rosy prospect. This is the risk that in making training more effective it may make it harder for the mentally handicapped person to be seen as a person and a subject, rather than an object for other people to practise on. Mannoni (1973) repeatedly refers to the fact that many mentally handicapped children are treated, and therefore behave, as objects. 'They are lived' by other people, especially their mothers. It is always difficult for a child to establish the boundaries between him- or herself and his or her mother; the bond between a mentally handicapped child and his or her mother is sometimes far stronger than the ordinary bond, for practical and emotional reasons, and there is often a special problem in detaching the child from the mother. Some of the symptoms of mentally handicapped children are therefore not inherent in the handicap itself, but arise from emotional factors in the family relationships. This point will be pursued in the next chapter.

Mannoni refers to the danger of technical re-education which ignores the personal life of the mentally handicapped person. This is not an attack on technical education itself, but it is a useful reminder of the need to wait and listen to what the person, who happens to be mentally handicapped, is experiencing – to respect his or her own initiative, and to restrain one's enthusiasm for producing change by external manipulation. Mannoni presents her book as an attempt to avoid 'a situation . . . in which parents, re-educators, and doctors, instead of trying to listen to the child as a desiring subject, integrate him as an object of treatment into various systems of social absorption and rob him of his speech' (p. xii).

Most social workers will find themselves in easy agreement with this as a general statement of aims, but it may nevertheless be difficult to live up to it. It is not only anxiety to train and educate that leads to neglect of the mentally handicapped person as a subject: many other kinds of social pressure can arise, at any stage of life.

*   *   *

The parents of a teenage girl were anxious to have her sterilised. The GP referred her to the appropriate surgeon, and it was only he (one is tempted to say 'of all people') who stopped the process in its tracks by insisting that he talk with the girl herself. He explained the implications of the operation to her and asked what she thought about it. Everyone present was astonished by the ordinariness of her answer: 'I'll have to talk with my boyfriend about that.'

*   *   *

Mentally handicapped people are often robbed of their speech because other people do not believe that they have ideas or that any ideas they might have would have any value; they do not allow time for halting or diffident expression, or are frightened of what the handicapped person might say. CMH has demonstrated, in its 'Participation' conferences, that mentally handicapped people do have an image of themselves, have views about how others treat them, can say what they think about their life and the world they are given to live it in, and are in touch with their own feelings.

Williams (1978) has pointed out that other people lack skills when it comes to talking with the mentally handicapped, and need to develop them. Sometimes only patience is needed; sometimes an interpreter, or special skill in using non-verbal techniques. If social workers are not to be wholly dependent on the prejudices and fixed ideas of others they have to learn these techniques, mostly by putting themselves in face-to-face contact more often with mentally handicapped people, until they have confidence in their clients' and their own ability to talk.

Anyone who is tempted to argue that this kind of issue is only relevant to the less severely handicapped should read Hales's *Children of Skylark Ward* (1978), by a teacher in a hospital school. In her group of seventeen children, aged from 2 to 18 only one had a few words, two were blind and three were partially sighted, two were deaf and many others had impaired hearing. All had cerebral palsy; nearly all had convulsions and were therefore on drugs which made them sleepy; most were doubly incontinent. Yet John (14) 'used his whole body to communicate. He could contract into a tight ball of rejecting disapproval; when pleased he waved his arms and kicked his legs with a strong rapid action' (pp. 9–10). And Hilda (10) 'loved minor disasters which involved the discomfiture of an adult, and this was a child whose mental level was assessed to be similar to that of a one-year-old (p. 15).

Hales stresses the importance of detailed observation and sensitivity to minute signals, like fleeting smiles. If reinforced these can become the vehicle for meaning and communication; and by a programme of tiny steps performance and language may be developed. She also stresses the importance for physically handicapped children of physical contact. They are not able, as other children are, to explore their own bodies and orientate themselves within them. It is therefore important for their carers and teachers to touch them and manipulate their limbs to increase their awareness of self and space. Communication at this physical level establishes the relationship out of which language may develop. As other writers have made clear (Newson *et al.*, 1979), the key questions are not 'How many words does this child have?' but 'How does he make his needs and wishes known?' and 'How do you persuade him to co-operate with you?' Pre-linguistic communication happens naturally with any tiny baby and his or her mother, and this is the starting-point for many handicapped children. Reciprocal body movements, like rocking, clapping or smiling, which show a readiness to play together, may start as 'mere' pleasure – self-rewarding – but as rituals are established, with one action regularly following another, this can lead to anticipation (the peep-bo response) and so to teasing and surprise. And as mutual sensitivity develops these actions can become symbolic gestures which convey meaning. They are essential 'vocabulary' if the mentally handicapped person is to be able to 'speak' back and not merely be the recipient of training communications from other people.

Another illustration of the value of letting mentally handicapped people speak for themselves was provided by a small project arranged by John Morton, the headmaster of a special school for ESN/S children. His report (1979) describes a venture in 'minimal intervention', when he lived for two weeks in a house with four of his pupils. Having recognised in his school 'many occasions on which there was a strong impulse to intervene, yet in most cases intervention was not necessary', he decided to let things take their course, as far as possible, except to prevent danger, avoid situations which got out of hand, or give help when directly requested if he thought it necessary. The result was that the children became much more communicative, talking more freely with one another than they would have done in school. They had difficulty at first in initiating activities, even when they had recognised their discomfort and the need for action ('I don't want to do nothing') but gradually started to act more freely, correcting and even directly teaching one another. The fact that adults were not controlling their time also meant that they were better able to assimilate what they were learning and to experiment with their new skills. They each developed special roles in the house, which were real and were reinforced by the approval of the group.

There is obviously a need for training, and a need for space of this kind — freedom from training. There is not an inevitable conflict between the two. There is no reason why many mentally handicapped people should not be fully involved in choosing the goals of training — agreeing what they want to learn. And even when this is difficult and the goals are self-evidently necessary — with road safety, perhaps, or personal hygiene — they can be encouraged to express their feelings about the training. The training itself, however, should be focused on clear goals, and 'powerfully' organised. The fact that it is a person who is receiving it should never be forgotten.

Society has been largely protected from the need to learn how to communicate with mentally handicapped people by the long history of segregation and specialisation in their services. Not the least of the revolutions of the last ten years has been a change in this. Mentally handicapped people have been more in the public eye, and something of the need to vary one's expectations — to understand behaviour differently — has begun to permeate society. This is the other side of the 'normalisation' discussion. It is usually concerned with helping mentally handicapped people to feel themselves to be normal and learn to behave conventionally, so that the rest of society comes to see them in a more ordinary light. It is equally important for the rest of society to recognise that mentally handicapped people have certain special needs and that these must be understood. Indeed normalisation cannot work unless this kind of sensitivity is developed in ordinary places. Since this is now such an important part of the new climate for mentally handicapped people, it is worth spending a little more time on the normalisation question.

Normalisation

Originally outlined by Bank-Mikkelsen, head of the Danish Mental Retardation Services in 1969, the main principles were described by Nirje (1970) as follows:

i   the mentally handicapped should experience the same rhythms of the day, week, year and life cycle as others,

ii   children should experience a normal family atmosphere,

iii   schools should cater for all children together,

iv   the problems of self-image of handicapped adults and of acceptance as adults by others should be tackled,

v   the handicapped should experience change (it is normal to move away from home in adolescence, for instance),

vi   in old age the connections with earlier life should not be severed,

vii   the viewpoint of the handicapped should be discovered and respected,

viii   the sexes should not be separated,

ix   the handicapped should receive and handle basic financial privileges,

x   the standards of their facilities should be modelled on those for the general population.

If these principles sound like common sense, that is only

because of the effectiveness of the normalisation campaign in the last decade. One does not have to search far to find settings — hospitals, of course, but also hostels, ATCs, special schools and families — where they are widely breached in practice, or to find services where the principles themselves are in dispute. Those who look after handicapped people are naturally anxious to protect them against danger. When they work in an hierarchical setting this protectiveness is reinforced by self-protectiveness; they are not free to take risks which may redound on their superiors, and they are nervous of criticism from them. When they are responsible for more handicapped people than they can reasonably supervise, they must fall back on avoidance of even simple risks if they are to keep catastrophe at bay. And when they believe that their jobs depend on the maintenance of a particular structure, then it becomes very hard to set change in motion. These are the fundamental reasons why caring people end up creating restrictive and stunting environments for the people they are trying to help. The handicapped then begin to react to that environment by ritualised behaviour and loss of personal initiative and spontaneity, and acquire a reputation for dependence and passivity, which justifies a protective environment. It is then very hard for the caring staff to believe that their charges could behave differently: their whole experience denies it. It needs something of a revolution to change perceptions, before organisational structures can change, and it is this that normalisation attempts.

By expecting conventional behaviour, caring people can both produce it and encourage others — society at large — to expect it; and so stigma is removed. This point has been made by Edgerton (1967), who argues that much eccentric behaviour is tolerated in people who are socially competent in other ways. By teaching competence in ordinary social skills, it is possible to mask peculiarities of physique, mental process or behaviour. By dressing well, knowing how to greet people and to manage bodily processes, the mentally handicapped can win social acceptance. This must, therefore, be an important aim of training.

This whole approach has now been elaborated by Wolfensberger (1972) and is becoming the current paradigm. But there is something of a paradox to be resolved in the reality that mentally handicapped people have special needs. The normalisation campaign has generated most heat in the field of special education. The philosophy of special schools rests on the belief that certain children benefit by being taken out of the ordinary school environment and placed in a setting, usually much more circumscribed and specialised than that of ordinary comprehensive or primary schools. But such schools separate their pupils from contact with ordinary school pupils and make it difficult for them to participate in the whole range of activities which go on in ordinary schools. In one sense, therefore, special schools make children different; but in another sense they make them more ordinary, by removing competitive pressures in which they will always lose the struggle: by making it possible for them to reward their teachers by their success and pleasure, and by enabling teachers to develop special sensitivity and skill. However, such specialisation can lead to underestimation of what can be achieved and the institutional cycle can commence again.

A very similar dilemma exists for social workers. Mentally handicapped people are often regarded as abnormal, and treated in stigmatising and rejecting ways. They are, therefore, appropriate candidates for social work help. But the attachment of a social worker to someone is in itself a stigmatising process and it becomes a matter of fine judgement whether social workers should seek to provide help themselves, or try to make it available through less stigmatising channels.

It should be a general principle of social work that every effort should be made to return clients to the ordinary networks of exchange and support on which their neighbours can depend. In this sense, as soon as society regards mentally handicapped people as having the same rights as other people, social workers will cease to be necessary. Thus it is highly appropriate for social workers to identify themselves with the normalisation campaign, not in the barren sense of driving mentally handicapped people out of the hospitals into an uncaring community, or out of special schools into insensitive educational emporia, but in the positive sense of working to create sensitive places for them in ordinary environments, so that the special ones may dissolve.

The social worker's experience

The relationship between a social worker and a mentally handicapped person may take several forms. Sometimes the main relationship is with the parents and contact with the mentally handicapped person is almost incidental. The social worker merely meets him or her in the course of discussing the parents' problems. Sometimes the social worker is thrust into a direct relationship by other people who want some problem solved, or merely want to see how the social worker copes. Sometimes, however, the relationship is an independent one, because the mentally handicapped person wants something from it. This is more likely to happen with adults, but this is by no means the only case.

In any of these situations various kinds of difficulties may arise. Some of these stem from the mentally handicapped person, some from the social worker and some from other people. We have already discussed some of the barriers to communication which are inherent in mental handicap itself, particularly the slow growth of language and concepts. But these are by no means closely associated with social skills and many mentally handicapped people are expert at managing other people, by conventional means or otherwise. This is true of the grossly handicapped as well as of the mildly handicapped. Indeed since many of those with extreme handicaps are found in institutional care, they have often developed extraordinary skill in manipulating their environment. McCormack (1979, pp. 36—7) describes Susan:

> not a pretty child, but a great giggler, very responsive and plainly everybody's favourite. Outsiders and ward staff alike tickle her and tease and play with her. She not only gets her share of mothering, but a bit of everyone else's as well.

Susan used techniques that are socially acceptable. Some mentally handicapped people, however, have learned that it is more effective to stir up trouble: people then pay more attention, even if it leads to disagreeable scenes. A little experience of working with children and being guided by one's own reactions helps to sort out what kind of game one is involved with. Much of the problem lies in one's own expectations. Certainly in the early days of working with mentally handicapped people, social workers do not know what to expect. Much of the difficulty in making contact comes from embarrassment and uncertainty. One is faced with a tiny pale figure in a wheelchair, who is said to be 14 but looks 7 and utters odd noises. Does one risk a complete sentence, stick with 'hello' or put out a tentative hand? A large grinning lad takes one's hand and draws one away to another room. Does he do this to everyone? Is he making one part of a stupid ritual or really trying to say something? Other people are often of little help in these situations: either they have not noticed the ambiguities, or they are amused to see how one copes. It is important, as in child psychiatry, to learn to live with these uncertainties for they gradually reveal what is going on. The embarrassment of parents or staff; the way they intervene; one's own feeling of sympathy, annoyance or depression; the reactions of siblings or fellow patients – any of these signs can tell a story if one is observant. But often one also has to act oneself: the situation is a social one and one has to convey willingness to understand and communicate. The only rational approach is an experimental one, to try in as clear a way as possible to convey a message – whether verbally or by gesture – and watch for a response. The tiny smiles or frowns that Hales (1978) spoke of can sometimes convey all that is needed, if one is open-minded enough to spot them and not too bound up in the conventions of ordinary language. As with a foreign language, the hardest part of communication is often to understand what is being said. If it is being said with painful determination or enormous gusto, but is totally obscure, the experience can be very stressful for the listener. The temptation is always to limit one's own discomfort by appealing to others for a translation, or by switching off completely. If one has ever watched a councillor visiting a home for the confused elderly or for very young children, one knows that for onlookers there is a certain savage pleasure in watching the struggle – which does not ease the actor's predicament. The rule, as in other situations, is that if one starts a communication, it should be followed through to a conclusion – until one understands what is being conveyed, or knows fairly surely that it is a meaningless ritual or a repetitive game.

This is by no means easy in many situations, especially those in which someone else is putting pressure on the social worker to resolve a crisis. When parents reach the end of their tether and want a child removed to residential care or hospital, it is essential to understand the *whole* of the situation, including the views of the mentally handicapped person at the focal point. It is hard enough to disentangle such 'extrusion' crises with families in which everyone can talk plain English. When the central character in the drama cannot use language at all effectively, resolution may be out of the question. This does not mean that it is not worth the effort of trying. The fact that it was assumed that he or she had a point of view is in itself an important message for all participants. Such crises can generate a good deal of guilt if they are taken only at face value, and this is one of the factors which lead to rejection of children or adults who are transferred abruptly to residential care. They have been depersonalised in the crisis itself; the services have seemed to confirm this evaluation and it becomes altogether too painful to reopen the personal issues — what he or she may have felt — afterwards. It is far better for this to be faced at the time of the crisis.

*   *   *

Tom lived with his father and mother until he was 38. Then his father died. He and his mother had to move then from their tied cottage, but they carried on together for twelve years. He was an odd fellow, who enjoyed frightening other people by suddenly shouting, and hung about the streets all day. When his mother fell ill, he went to the local hospital for a month. She was looked after at home, and in Tom's absence the neighbours told her how disagreeable they found him and how they dreaded his return. His mother was very shocked to hear this because she had never suspected it, and refused to have him home. Eventually he was given a place in an old people's home! No one ever spoke with the neighbours. His mother found visits to the home very painful because she could not explain to Tom why she had decided that he must stay away. She gradually stopped visiting. Even after seven years Tom is still grieving and keeps his suitcase packed for when his mother will come for him.

*   *   ,   *

There are other ways in which third parties can make it hard for a social worker and a mentally handicapped person to communicate effectively. Parents or staff who speak for him or her are a common example. They are sometimes so discomfited by the awkwardness and unsociability of their charge that they find it hard even to let the social worker suffer. It is often tempting again to take this at face value, accepting that they probably do know best and that the alternative is not likely to be very productive. The pattern has probably been established so long that the mentally handicapped person is trained to have no awareness of his or her own views, and one visit will not change that. But it is never a waste of time to try and get a response, provided one really wants one. Surprisingly often, if one's own communication is clear and emphatic and not merely a ritual, there is an unexpected reaction; and with the less severely handicapped it can be startlingly helpful.

*   *   *

Maureen was a large 13 year old and clung to her mother. Her mother one day wrote to the social services department to say that Maureen must go away, but when the social worker called to see her she could give no reason why this was suddenly necessary. When the social worker began to talk about the effect of a mentally handicapped child on a marriage, however, she became very tense. Maureen also stopped moving around. the social worker asked her, 'What's the matter, Maureen?'; and she went across to her mother and said, 'Don't cry'. Her mother burst into tears, and gradually revealed that she was frightened that Maureen's growing womanhood would come between her and her husband. She was also frightened that the close bond between herself and Maureen would be destroyed. This began a useful family discussion about how she had kept Maureen to herself and had encouraged her husband to separate himself off in the early days after Maureen was born. Maureen's simple intervention was pivotal in opening this up.

*   *   *

Those who live with a mentally handicapped person almost inevitably fall into ways of relating which cut off communication in certain ways, denying that he or she has feelings about awkward subjects: about the way others treat him or her, about relationships between staff or parents, about sexual feelings or leisure activities. It makes life seem more manageable if such feelings are kept at bay. If someone like a social worker then starts lifting lids it can be very threatening to a whole lifestyle.

Adolescence and sex

Adolescence is the time when this type of problem appears most clearly. Some mentally handicapped 'children' then need help to find their own voices. Like all adolescents they begin to see things differently from their parents. This problem is not one of mental handicap but it is exacerbated by their lack of social skills and by the protectiveness of their parents. Most teenagers have difficulty in finding ways of exploring their sexual feelings without generating a good deal of anxiety in their parents. It requires a good deal of skill and ingenuity to find opportunities and unsupervised areas, even if they have a willing partner. The mentally handicapped teenager not only lacks this kind of skill, but is often under much closer parental supervision and may have fewer opportunities to find co-operative partners. To help with this kind of problem is not easy, because it means that everyone involved has to face their sexual attitudes much more squarely than usual. Sexual behaviour is usually regarded as a private matter, even in 'liberated' circles, and the skills needed are not much talked about. It would not be easy if it were just a matter of the social worker and the mentally handicapped person talking together, but it is usually infinitely harder because parents and others are involved. One of the ways in which mentally handicapped people do not fit the norms of our society is that there is no clear way of defining when they are able to make their own decisions and be free of parental or family supervision.

*   *   *

Jean, who is 43, lives in a group home and has a part-time job as a mother's help. She cooks and cleans in the house and manages her own clothes. Her sister, who is 38, calls to see her weekly, and it was only after six months that the social worker discovered that the sister was controlling Jean's money for her. When asked about it, she said she had assumed that Jean could not handle her own money and she had felt responsible. She was rather indignant that the social services should 'take it on themselves to handle Jean's affairs' and was surprised at the idea that Jean could decide for herself how her money should be spent, and who should help her with it.

*   *   *

How much more of a problem an adolescent's body would have been!

Residential social workers, nurses and staff in ATCs will be familiar with this problem. Do they have freedom to work out solutions to the problems of their residents on the basis of the residents' own choices, or are they constrained by the wishes of relatives as well? For school teachers the issue is clearer because their pupils are minors, but they too may feel some difficulty if they develop a programme to which some parents might take exception. Parents are often very willing to talk about this subject, if the first layers of reserve can be peeled away. They have many common anxieties, which it is a relief to share, in a privileged setting. Some of these concern the maintenance of ordinary social norms: preventing their children from causing embarrassment or annoyance to others by masturbating in public; being too exuberant in their demonstrations of affection; or assuming the licence of infants when they are physically adult. Some are to do with actual danger: of girls becoming pregnant or being misused by others, or of boys making apparently sexual advances to children. Some are concerned with giving their children as full a life as possible: helping them to discover their own bodies and to find acceptable ways of getting pleasure from them.

There are attitudes to sex which cannot be entirely reconciled: the view that a sexual relationship is only morally right within marriage or that everyone is entitled to a sexual life, whatever his or her marital state, for instance. This is an area in which battles are being fought in society as a whole: the norms are not clear, and a good deal of anxiety comes from the fact that no one really knows what the rules are.

There are those who argue that mentally handicapped people have no sexual needs, unless they are aroused by others; and that it is no kindness to make them aware of needs they can never satisfy. We must obviously beware of generalisations in this area, as in others: we are talking about a wide range of personal development and social awareness. It is not uncommon, even in these situations, to find that masturbation or covert flirtatiousness is common knowledge, and that this is regarded as 'fairly normal' and 'not what we are talking about'. Often, however, the same people are known in another setting − the ATC, perhaps, or a youth club − to engage in sexual by-play, phantasies or indeed relationships, which are unknown to their primary carers. It may then be quite shocking to the latter when the truth comes out.

Many mentally handicapped adults do not seem to have fully developed adult sexual needs; they behave more like children in the latency period, unaware of the double meanings their behaviour may have for others. It may be true that their needs are more for physical comfort and reassurance than for genital satisfaction. This applies as much to apparently homosexual as to heterosexual behaviour. But it is hard with this group to know whether their stage of development is a maturational one or one that has been learned socially. Especially with those who have had long experience in institutions, one cannot ignore the repressive effect of other people's morality.

Many parents who can recognise that their children have sexual needs and interests, are nevertheless very worried about it. They sense that there are strong resistances in society to open recognition that handicapped people have such needs; they know that the lack of social skills in their children will lead to frustration; and they find themselves faced with dilemmas which are taxing and uncharted in ordinary folk-lore. Whether they are worried by sexual behaviour itself, the likely reaction of other people, by dangers of possible pregnancy or fears of what a deepening relationship could mean for them and their child, they get little help. It is not surprising then, that some try to limit their anxiety by early repression and that some mentally handicapped people then develop compensatory behaviour which may itself be disturbing.

*   *   *

Sandra was a normal-looking girl although her IQ was only in the fifties. At the age of 14 she started following a neighbour's teenage son around, to his and her parents' embarrassment. They tried to divert her at first and then kept her indoors when he was likely to be around. Sandra started to be ill-tempered and unco-operative. On two occasions she came downstairs with no clothes on and threw a tantrum when her parents tried to make her dress again. Finding that this produced a strong reaction, she tried the same game at school and was hit by one of the other girls who was very shocked. She also began to have fits of weeping at school and at home. Although the neighbour's son was in their home occasionally, Sandra seemed to have lost interest in him. She improved greatly some weeks later when her father bought her a bicycle.

*   *   *

In this case it is far from clear that Sandra's behaviour was sexually determined, at least by her, and it might have been easier for everyone if it had been possible to treat it more lightly, as a question of appropriate manners. Even in other cases where the sexual component is evident, parental attitudes may be the most critical factor.

*   *   *

Peter, at the age of 16 started to make comments to older women about their appearance and his behaviour towards his mother became much more amorous. Deserted by her husband when Peter was only 8 years old, she had brought him up with his younger brother and sister with considerable difficulty, and was often frightened of his growing strength. She still bathed him herself, though increasingly embarrassed by his occasional erections and display of himself. One day, when he had made a nuisance of himself at a picnic by raising the skirts of one of his mother's friends — causing some amusement but a number of red faces — his mother told him angrily that he must never do it again. The next day he somehow got into the bathroom when she was having a bath, and refused to leave until she got out and pushed him out. He also frightened her by half-pulling her into his own bath a night or two later. Peter regarded both episodes as very funny and recounted them to the ATC staff each time. His mother was considerably disturbed by them and called to see the social worker to ask if Peter was becoming a danger to others, and whether he would be better off in institutional care. In discussion, her own loneliness was unmistakable and her dilemma in handling Peter acutely difficult. If she was to correct him she had to speak harshly to him and could not then tolerate his miserable behaviour.

But any attempt by her to make reparation provoked him into an amorous display, which she had once enjoyed but was now afraid of.

*   *   *

In both these cases the social worker would usually be involved in helping the parents to disentangle their own problems of handling the child; but in this context we must also ask the question: how can Sandra and Peter best be helped? They are each strong individuals who are trying to adjust the world to meet needs, which they find it hard to put into words. To think straight about them one has to look squarely at them as potential sexual beings and grasp the meaning of their behaviour in *their* terms, not in terms of conventional adult projections. This in turn probably means getting to know them as individuals. It has to be possible at the same time to think of Sandra as a developing seductress or seducer's victim, and as a child playing the games that best attract adult attention to her. It is not good enough to dismiss the first hypothesis, not only because one would then fail to grasp her parents' anxieties, but because it may have truth in it. But it is also unsatisfactory to behave as if it alone were true. Sandra is the only person who could explain where the meaning lay for her and it would require skill to help her to explain – skill which could probably only come through an established relationship in which her idioms came to be understood. Indeed, Sandra herself may be looking for the meaning of her own feelings. It is possible, with too hasty a reaction, to impose a one-dimensional adult view, which actually makes her behaviour frightening to herself and her self-image a 'bad' one.

With Peter too, the special mixture of developing male and reactive boy had to be teased out. He is not just a cause of anxiety to others, but a whole person who is discovering his strengths and perplexities and for whom words may not be an easy currency for working these problems out. It is trite to say that if his mother's situation had been easier – if she had been comfortable with her own sexuality – she would probably have handled the situation better, and Peter would have learned more quickly where his limits lay. Social workers are rarely asked to help with ideal situations, but with real people in disintegrating worlds. Peter's mother needed reassurance and help to sort out her own problems, but Peter also needed help. In this case the removal of his mother's anxiety — bringing the facts out into the open and removing the guilt — might have settled things down enough for common sense to take over; in other cases it might be necessary to work out a range of ways to set limits without provoking too much reaction; in some a period of residential care might be best, to allow someone else to set new patterns. The central point is that Peter's own system of meaning is as important for deciding what to do, as the systems of the other people round him. When the social worker is charged with finding a way through the tangle of difficulties, he or she needs to be able to communicate with Peter directly. This is as true of the difficulties experienced by mentally handicapped people in hospitals or schools as of those at home, and over problems of work or domestic management or leisure as in sexual behaviour.

A good deal of sanity and openness has been brought to the question of the sexuality of mentally handicapped people by Ann and Michael Craft (1978 and 1979). They provide an excellent review of the subject, and remove any lingering doubt that mentally handicapped people have ordinary feelings and a capacity for love and mutuality. Their many illustrations of couples who have made successful marriages are a loud warning that we should not interfere too readily with developing relationships. Marriage brought a great improvement in the quality of life for nearly all those who undertook it, even if it was not without problems. More importantly, perhaps, they dispel a good deal of the anxiety, for parents and residential staff, which surrounds the issue of sex, by looking squarely at the questions. Since so much of the problem is rooted in the attitudes of carers, it can be very useful to arrange a series of discussions from time to time, in each area, and perhaps an occasional workshop on the model of the Castle Priory conferences (Castle Priory College, Wallingford, Oxon OX10 0HE), so that care staff can share with one another and with parents the value judgements which they otherwise make secretly, and anxiously. It will not be possible to formulate any rules because the situation of *each mentally handicapped person* must be reviewed separately, but at least it should be possible to check the available options.

Work

One of the ways in which the development of mentally handicapped adolescents may be restricted is by carers assuming that they will not be able to get or keep a job. There are many reasons, in the present economic climate, for pessimism on the statistical level: it will be difficult for the majority of mentally handicapped people. On the individual level this does not necessarily apply; and there is considerable work to be done in dispelling the belief of employers that mentally handicapped workmen and women are not competitive with others. A number of studies have appeared recently which make it clear that many more mentally handicapped people could be employed if they were trained in specific tasks, properly analysed to be within their capacity. It has been suggested that up to 95 per cent of those with Down's Syndrome could be employed; whereas many ATC instructors would say that virtually none of their trainees could be. This difference is explained by different beliefs about the efficacy and availability of training. Lane (1980) concluded that guardians (parents, teachers, instructors, doctors) of adults with Down's Syndrome seek a caring rather than an independent environment; and that gatekeepers to employment (careers officers and disablement resettlement officers) believed that Down's Syndrome sufferers were a homogeneous group 'requiring care and being incapable of employment' (p. 42). There is every reason to think that these attitudes would apply equally to other groups of mentally handicapped adults.

The Pathway Scheme of the NSMHC, which has provided a work training scheme for mentally handicapped people in Wales since 1975, has proved that even very severely handicapped people can hold down jobs. The scheme designs an individual social, educational and training programme for each trainee, covering all the skills likely to be needed in a normal work setting, from clocking in to talking to the boss and being teased. The actual training may take place in an ATC, a further education college or a special training unit. The trainee is then placed with a 'foster worker' in a real job — an important innovation which continues the training process, removes minor difficulties and often creates a friendship. Employers are given a training grant for a probationary period if they require it, and the trainee receives a full rate for the job. A placement officer stays in contact with the worker and his or her family for a long period. What the scheme demonstrates is that if each problem which usually bars the way to successful employment is tackled carefully and completely, then mentally handicapped people can become very successful employees, with a productivity rate often quite as good as that of other employees, and with far fewer problems of sickness and disaffection. Another approach which has proved very successful, when a sympathetic employer can be found, is to create an 'enclave' within a factory or workshop – a whole work-group of mentally handicapped people who, with their own supervisor, undertake a particular function or set of tasks, perhaps on a contract basis, for an ordinary wage in an ordinary setting.

Many of these issues are analysed by Whelan and Speake (1981), who give clear and practical advice for ATC staff and others who want to take seriously the employment of the mentally handicapped. Even the present economic situation need not depress them in their task of proving – and perhaps first discovering – that mentally handicapped people, properly trained, can make wholly satisfactory workers. In spite of government publicity, like the leaflet 'Employing Someone who is Mentally Handicapped' (ESA, 1976) and earlier work (Tuckey *et al.*, 1973), this point has not yet been accepted.

Independent living: group homes and flats

It is easier to think about the mentally handicapped person as an independent agent when he or she is in a situation of independence – living outside institutional or family care. The growing body of experience of helping mentally handicapped people, whether brought up in hospital or at home, to move into a place of their own, to survive and to establish themselves as individuals, is one of the most exciting chapters in recent history. The following account of what this kind of life means to an individual illustrates the real impact of institutions:

*　　　*　　　*

It is the little things I like — being able to switch off my own light, or coming home with a bag of chips I don't have to explain to anyone. Or if someone knocks the door, I mean it makes me nervous, but I know it has got to do with me. The other day a man came. I didn't know him, but he was like lost and wanted to know how to get to Philip Street. Well I go past that way often, so I told him, and when I shut the door I thought, 'Yes, this is my place: I can tell people about it now.'

*　　　*　　　*

This is the direct voice of someone in her own flat for the first time in her life and clearly expanding with every day. A similar note is struck by those in group homes, even if they had reservations about going there. One told her social worker:

*　　　*　　　*

I wasn't for leaving the hospital at first, you know. They said 'Go on; give it a try'; and I thought they would just push us out and forget us. Well, perhaps they have, but it don't matter now. You'd not think four people could hit it off the way we have. I won't say we don't ever niggle, but it blows over ever so quick really. What makes me feel so good is when I put my key in the lock and think, 'They can't do this up the hospital, and even Sister Reilly can't do it down here either.' I am the fairy queen here.

*　　　*　　　*

Others might put the emphasis on buying their own food, staying in bed as long as they want, being greeted by the neighbours, going down to the pub, having friends in, breaking their own china, collecting personal possessions or getting a pet. The extent to which these small incidents of daily life come under the control of an independent resident is hard to see from inside an institution; and it is impossible to know which will prove an important stimulus and which an impossible hurdle.

The selection and preparation of people for group homes and other forms of independent living is likely to be a vital role for social workers in the next ten years, as the run-down of the hospitals continues. In this role there will be a number of issues to consider. The first group home in an area is likely to be surrounded by all sorts of hopes and fears, and it will not always be easy to protect it and its residents against external projections of this kind. There are likely to be fears among neighbours. Fortunately, a group home run as a single household without resident staff, will usually be accepted as an ordinary household for planning purposes and will not require consent for change of use. Local people quickly pick up rumours, however, and may start to campaign against the home. It is usually better to respond to actual anxiety or hostility than to try to anticipate it, because the latter course of action often seems to provoke as much anxiety as it allays. The technique which seems to have been most successful is finding a local ally — a neighbour, preferably next door — who is kept fully informed and through whom information is filtered to other neighbours. By asking such a person to hold the key for tradesmen, one can make it easy for the house to be looked over by local people and provide an immediate point of contact for future residents when they come to see the house. On one notable occasion the neighbour's children were to be seen playing in the garden on the day when residents moved in, making it very hard for other people's anxiety to survive.

Another group who may be anxious are the parents of mentally handicapped adults who are either in need of residential care or have been kept inappropriately in hospital. The group home, especially if it is the first in the area, may become a symbol for many frustrations. It carries the implication that mentally handicapped people can do more for themselves than has been allowed; and over protective parents may have to accept that they might have done things better in the past. It may also seem to imply that the local authority is unwilling to recognise the need for staffed hospitals. Taken together, these two themes can provoke considerable opposition, and an over-involved interest in what goes on in the home. Nothing is worse for people who have newly gained their independence than to find they are living in a goldfish bowl; and the social worker is likely to have to play a vigorous role in discouraging too many official visitors and inspections.

This role is often misunderstood, and it is usually necessary to insist time and again on the right of the residents to the privacy they pay for in their rent. Their contract will usually be an ordinary landlord/tenant one, which makes their home a private dwelling and themselves masters or mistresses of the threshold. Councillors will often take this point faster than parents or other professionals (nurses from the hospital perhaps), who have been both concerned in preparing people for residence and anxious about the outcome. It may also be necessary to recognise one's own anxiety to protect, and indeed the willingness of residents to be over-protected.

The excellent Operational Policy document, prepared in 1976 by Cardiff University's Social Services for its group home project, deals (among its ninety-six points!) with the same issues of visiting and protectiveness:

[Point] 82. Visitors concerned with the theory, principles or operation of the home shall not be permitted to visit except in the most exceptional circumstances with the full agreement of all the residents.

87. The social worker shall visit the home for a period which will not normally exceed ten hours in any one week.

The Cardiff project, with its involvement of non-handicapped residents, is a very special one, but puts its emphasis squarely on training and the creation of a 'normal' environment. It is paradoxical in one sense to suggest that training and normality can coexist: the statistical norm is one of exposed independence. But for those with special needs there is obviously a gap to be filled: the only question is whether it should be filled with protection alone, or with something more dynamic which allows the gradual development of self-reliance and the gradual removal of external supports. Some social workers, working with those in group homes, will find it difficult to limit their own need to protect, and hard to set appropriate educational goals. It is valuable to attempt to set out, as concretely as possible, the function it is hoped residents will be performing in six months' time, and the skills they will need in order to achieve this. It may then become much clearer whether these expectations are realistic, or whether too many tasks are being set at once; and how best to insert effective training – for instance, whether the ATC have a role, or parents or neighbours, or specially recruited volunteers.

Some of these issues are also likely to appear in the selection of residents. 'Don't assess: train' is a maxim that Marc Gold and others have preached, and this is highly relevant to selection for group homes. It is exceptionally difficult to know how someone will cope in a setting of independence until they have tried it, and no one has suggested an assessment mechanism which can guarantee success. What is more important is to provide training in everyday skills and exposure to the other potential residents. These can be conveniently combined in a training house or flat, which could be established in the community itself; in association with a hostel; in the grounds of a hospital; near an ATC; or even near a special school. In a setting which is not expected to be permanent it may be possible for people to take risks – to try things out in a relaxed way and find out whether they could cope with real independence. Some of the more able find that they do not have the courage; and some of the less able find a motivation for learning.

Sometimes this first training task will be the responsibility of people other than the social worker who provides support for group homes. If this is the case, it is important to ensure that the training is organised to take account of the actual environment of the home, and the philosophy on which it has been set up. It is not unusual for future residents to be trained to use a cooker of a type which cannot be put into their home; or to be taught a routine for shopping in a supermarket when their local shop is not self-service. Similarly they may be encouraged to telephone for help at all hours, when the real situation will preclude this, and they will be expected to save problems until certain fixed times. Or the group may be allowed to depend too heavily on the leadership and initiative of one member, when this will be discouraged later by the social worker.

These misalignments can to some extent be avoided if the social worker is involved in the planning of the training programme from the beginning; but in some areas it has been found best to organise the main training in the actual group home, where it can be related firmly to reality from start to finish. There is a good deal to be said for this approach, but it may be harder to free staff to do it if they are required to keep an eye on other programmes at the same time. It should not need saying, but usually does, that the prospective residents must be closely involved in the planning of their own training. They are individuals with personal wishes for their own future and particular worries about the move they are about to make. When John reveals that he plans to have a bicycle, a whole set of training needs is suddenly apparent: new road safety issues, handling security locks, finding a cycle shop and so on. If Emily can be encouraged to talk about her sudden obsession with lipstick, she may make it clear how frightened she is of answering the door – in case the police have come for her! The way in which this planning is done will depend on the kind of life they lead already. If they are together in one place it may be possible to arrange to talk over meals with staff they know already. If they live in separate places it may be necessary to start by talking with individuals and their families (brothers and sisters can often help to point up hopes and fears which are not obvious to all), and later bring them together with the trainers, whoever they may be. This process is by no means a ritual: if residents are to be ready to take decisions for themselves, they have to see themselves as decision-makers as soon as possible.

Living alone

Some mentally handicapped people are already out on their own when social workers first encounter them. Some have been stranded by accidents in the family – the death of parents perhaps, or the onset of some disabling condition on top of their mental handicap. They may suddenly come to light because of a minor incident involving the police or a neighbour's complaint. Sometimes it is extraordinary how such people have managed to survive in appalling conditions.

*   *   *

One old man in his 70s had been living in a cottage from which the thatch had been disappearing for years. The living quarters were soaked whenever it rained and he simply retreated to his kitchen. He lived largely off vegetables which neighbours gave him, and only drew his pension occasionally. He had lived like this since the removal to hospital of his older brother twelve years previously; but no one seemed to have notified the mental welfare department or the social services until a fire damaged the remains of his roof. It then became possible to provide him with a caravan on his own land, and a home help to teach him how to improve his comforts.

*   *   *

Stories like this remind one both that there are caring people in the community besides social workers, and that these caring people can sometimes fade away imperceptibly, so that no one else notices that a gap has been left. Often in such situations there is a history of misunderstandings: siblings who gave the impression that they resented interference from neighbours but did nothing themselves; or a reputation for aggression or eccentricity that has kept people at bay. Individuals thus become anomalous and are left out of the network of exchange on which ordinary social life is built. This is exactly where social workers should come in — where common sense is not enough — and their task is first to try to re-establish the exchange links that are broken. This means locating relatives — emotionally as much as geographically; alerting the local vicar, health visitor and whoever else may be responsive; finding out what has happened with neighbours in recent months; and, of course, discovering what the client has himself to offer in return. A good social worker should be able to pick up threads like these with a little imagination, even if he or she has little knowledge of the area. But one must be aware that the wider the area one serves, the less effective one's contacts are likely to be at local level. Specialist social workers may therefore need to work in alliance with more local 'generic' workers, to pick up leads that are less evident: perhaps an old lady who once knew the family, or a young couple who are keen to do some voluntary work. The generic social worker, on the other hand, if the referral came to him or her, might well need to call on the experience of the mental handicap specialist, to sort out ways of teaching new skills or the meaning of angry outbursts.

Married couples and families

Finally, there are the mentally handicapped people who manage to fit in with the 'normal' marital and family pattern that surrounds them. Most social workers will have met parents where one or other parent has been at a special school or in a mental handicap hospital. Sometimes they have problems (otherwise the social worker would be unlikely to meet them); often they are managing quite well and their children are like other children. It always causes great anxiety, however, when two mentally handicapped people fall in love and propose to marry. Those responsible for their support usually feel they should try to discourage them, and feel a weight of social disapproval if they are unable or unwilling to succeed in this. The old eugenics fears are still active. There is little information available about the whole range of such marriages, but from what evidence there is one must conclude that many are successful in providing mutual support, comfort and companionship. Thirty-two couples were interviewed by Mattinson (1970) in which both partners had been diagnosed mentally handicapped and had been admitted to a hospital for mentally handicapped people at some time. Seventeen of the thirty-two couples had had children together — a total of forty children in all. Her findings accord with those of the Crafts (1979) and others:

1. that the success of the marriage has no direct correlation with the degree of handicap;
2. that the average number of children is lower than in the population as a whole;
3. that marriage has brought considerable enrichment to most couples' lives;
4. but that there is a need for support services for many, and in particular for sexual counselling.

As suggested earlier there is a clear need for professionals to be more aware of their own attitudes to sexual issues, so that they can give frank advice to mentally handicapped people and their relatives; or at least can ensure that they are put in touch with others who can supply this service. In some areas the Family Planning Association has taken a lead both in counselling the handicapped and in providing training for professionals who wish to become more effective in their own work. The staff at Castle Priory College have also taken an interest in this work recently, and have organised training programmes for parents and professionals together. Sexual and marital counselling are probably the most neglected areas still in the support of mentally handicapped couples. They are exposed to as much sexually provocative material as other people; but it is likely that many of them do not absorb even the minimal information given to children by their parents, school teachers or friends. Most mentally handicapped people also have fewer opportunities to experiment before marriage. Many will therefore have considerable areas of ignorance about both physiology and emotions, which must be filled.

These are not the only areas of ignorance. Social workers should be especially careful to check that their clients are aware of the usual sources of help, know their entitlement to social security and health services, and are able to make application themselves. The innumerable challenges of bureaucracy – income tax returns, census forms, rates bills, hire purchase agreements and so on – can cause great anxiety, and even simple letters can cause confusion.

The greatest distress, however, is caused by inadequate child care. In the present climate of unrest about non-accidental injury and child neglect, mentally handicapped parents can sometimes be very vulnerable. They often come from homes where there has been significant emotional stress; some have been rejected; some have had periods in residential care; few have had experience of looking after young children; training for parenthood at school has often been non-existent; tolerance of frustration may be low; ability to learn from experience is likely to be lower than average; and facility in making friends may also be reduced.

This is not to imply that all couples will be like this, and there is no reason to suppose that instinctual protectiveness towards children will be reduced. If it is so, it is an argument not for preventing marriage and childbearing, and not for such visits of inspection that self-confidence is eroded in an atmosphere of mutual suspicion, but for a full-scale programme of education for parenthood, which begins early in the marriage (or cohabitation), which has clear goals and standards to be achieved, and which creates a supportive relationship with someone who is likely to provide continuity over a number of years. This is the idea of the health visitor service, but it cannot be assumed that it will work out so well. Yet, unless something of this kind can be built up, there will be more cases like that of Helen.

*   *   *

Helen was so disturbed by the age of 12 that she was kept in an ESN/S school, and regarded there as very disruptive. She also began to have epileptic fits. At 15 she was often missing from home, and developed an attachment to a divorced man of 32, who seemed to have a calming influence on her, though emotionally immature himself. They married when she was 17 and very soon she was pregnant, though this was not brought to the notice of her GP for six months. The district nurse found her very alarming and they developed a mutual hostility which made any effective contact impossible. The GP managed to persuade her husband that she should go into hospital a week before the baby was due and a son was safely delivered. The hospital discharged them with great reluctance and the health visitor called twice a day at first. Conditions were chaotic: there was often no heating in November and December and food was erratic. By paying close attention to Helen's own feelings, and retaining her husband's goodwill, the health visitor kept access open for three months. The baby did not thrive, and towards the end of February was found blue with cold and some scarring under the hairline. He was removed to a place of safety, and Helen warned the health visitor never to reappear. For the next eighteen months the SSD kept the baby in foster care and Helen was allowed to visit him at the foster home. She became quite attached to the foster mother, and seemed to learn something of baby care. She was allowed to take the baby home for the day on two occasions but on the second refused to return him, and only the threat of legal action made her husband hand him over. Helen became very depressed at this time, as it was made increasingly clear that the baby would be kept in care. She was twice admitted to mental hospital. Six months later she was again pregnant. As soon as the baby was born, he was taken into care. Helen smashed her house up, and two days later threw herself under a lorry and was killed.

*   *   *

This is an extreme and appalling case and it is possible that no amount of support and education, even at the right time, would have made a difference for Helen. But it is futile to suggest that she should not have married or had children. There was no way she could have been prevented from doing so, sooner or later. The question is whether her difficulties should have been foreseen at an early enough stage to win her co-operation with a programme of support. Society, including its professionals, often seems merely to hope that nothing will happen – 'We don't want to seem to encourage her to have children' – and is then left only with strategies of control and self-protection, which are experienced as fault-finding when the unthinkable happens. Yet the ways of helping people like Helen were identified in the 1950s by Family Service Units and the NSPCC. They showed that it was possible, by a real identification with their clients, to win trust and co-operation, which is the prerequisite for effective support. This tradition has rarely thrived in the setting of local authority social work, in part because of the inescapable 'police' function of the local authority, and in part because resources were rarely made available for those with fewest personal strengths to call on.

Advocacy

Mentally handicapped people are much better able to speak for themselves than is often allowed. Because they are not allowed, however, they need help to raise their voices. Because those who look after them professionally, however benevolent, also have interests of their own, they do not do this reliably. It has therefore been suggested recently that they need independent advocates, who can make it their task to understand the world through the eyes of the person they represent, and to claim from it all the entitlements which belong to him or her. The idea of advocacy originated in America, where it sprang naturally from the 'rights' approach to welfare. But it is not merely a defensive strategy, to prevent intrusion on civil liberties: it is a positive strategy, to obtain help and opportunities of every kind – financial, therapeutic, educational – and access to accommodation, leisure, privacy and friendship. The idea of advocacy has its clearest application in large institutions, where it can be shown that mentally handicapped patients or residents have no one wholly devoted to their interests, but comprise a group of people with low status and power in a hierarchy of others. In Great Britain an Advocacy Alliance has recently been formed by the Spastics Society, MENCAP, MIND, One-to-One and the Cheshire Foundation. It is based at MIND and has already won the co-operation of some large hospitals for its programme of attaching trained voluntary advocates to individual people, who otherwise receive no visits from relatives or friends. The One-to-One programme first developed by Kith and Kids in 1970 was one precursor — attaching an individual volunteer for a day to mentally handicapped children — and this has been taken up by many hospitals as an occasional project, but the Advocacy Alliance promises to reach into far more areas of patients' lives, and to provide a structure for continuing relationships. Social workers have often seen the need to represent mentally handicapped people and have occasionally managed to play this role effectively. The Child Protection rules actually lay an obligation on SSDs to supervise children in hospital who are not in regular contact with their families, but this is often ignored. They have a complex role to play, which has to have regard for parents' interests and for their professional relationship with colleagues in other services. Often this makes it hard for them to be single-minded in the pursuit of one client's interests. There can therefore only be a welcome from them to the arrival of advocates who will range themselves alongside mentally handicapped individuals. This is a significant step towards normalisation, and it is to be hoped that social workers will lend their support to this latest venture in relating to mentally handicapped people. Advocacy, or Citizen Advocacy as it is known in the US, is not something to be undertaken lightly, and social workers will be familiar with many of the problems advocates are likely to encounter in trying to act honestly for another person, with commitment and consistency. For those who would like to know more about it, references will be found under Wolfensberger in the bibliography.

3

Relating to Parents

People are usually first labelled 'mentally handicapped' when they are children — often tiny infants. Even when the diagnosis is made later their parents are usually at the centre of the drama and social workers often deal almost exclusively with them. Certainly most of the accounts written by social workers about mental handicap have been about parents and their problems. This phenomenon is so obvious that it seems to need no explanation, but it is worth recognising what forces are at work to make it so.

First, society places great value on the parental role, and defends the rights of parents to control their children's fate by a whole battery of laws. This is not the whole story, however, because other laws and administrative arrangements make it possible for doctors, teachers, social workers and others to make decisions about children which may override their parents' wishes. There is a good deal of confusion about this, because of the difficulty of defining good parenting and children's needs; and the recent eruptions over child abuse have done little to clarify when parents are responsible and when society should intervene. Second, mentally handicapped children are less able to speak for themselves than other children, and depend more heavily on others, especially their parents, for help with ordinary living. Third, it suits society very well to leave damaged children in the care of their parents. It does not then have to provide for their (very expensive) care, and can avoid facing some of the moral dilemmas which such children present.

So the burden falls squarely on the parents, who are rarely

prepared for it, and it is not surprising that many of them experience acute disturbance and many have their lives distorted.

Getting the message

Nothing in our culture prepares young parents for the arrival of a damaged child; or perhaps it would be truer to say that our society works very hard to repress from consciousness the dark hints that it does give. We do have fairy stories about changeling children; old wives' tales about the effects of shock or bad dreams in pregnancy; we treat pregnant women as if they were in danger; but the conscious message is that babies are good, birth is a happy event, motherhood gives status, fathering is power. It seems sacrilegious and malevolent to ask parents-to-be: 'What will you do if your child is handicapped?' Yet the question needs asking. One in 250 babies is severely mentally handicapped, and the dice rolls rather evenly across the population.

Most parents are not just unprepared for a bad event: they are especially keyed up for a good one. If they have worries, they are about physical safety and pain. Then, at the moment when these worries are lifted and they let themselves relax, some of them are pole-axed. They are faced with terrifying questions about themselves, about one another, and about their future; they have to make moral choices about another life, in a glare of publicity and in a society which offers conflicting advice. Some can cope: they have accepted that life is sometimes very rough; they trust one another; they have good supporters; they get fairly coherent advice; they make time for themselves to think; they are in touch with their feelings; and they take the decisions as they come. For some again, the news breaks slowly, as their child does not quite do what is expected, and arouses questions, doubts and hesitant conclusions. But for the majority learning that their child is handicapped comes as a staggering blow. Hannam (1975) makes this very clear and also that the blow has often been made worse by the way in which it was delivered. First, however, let us consider what the message means.

All parents see themselves in their children. They look at their children through the experience they themselves have had – of a happy childhood they would have liked to continue, or of the losses, deprivations and failures they have suffered. They hope that they can live through their children and get satisfactions that have previously eluded them. At the same time they hope to be effective parents, creating new life and watching it grow under their care to independence. For the mother particularly there is a special bond – of having carried the child inside herself, knowing that it was part of her, its life dependent on hers; and of having experienced quite physically and directly its separation from her. It is hard for all children as they grow older to carry these projections from their parents, but normal children do not immediately challenge their parents' hopes. A seriously handicapped child fails to reflect the image that its parents project: it becomes an alien from the start (hence the changeling theme), something they cannot identify with; it fails to fill the gaps they have carried forward from their own childhoods. Or, if they have been seriously deprived themselves, the child may symbolise the gaps they are carrying inside themselves. What is more, in the first case, since they cannot avoid recognising that the child is part of them, it is as if they cannot identify with part of themselves: the mother's horror is made worse because the child came out of herself. These themes are sensitively discussed by Mannoni (1973) for anyone who is not allergic to psychoanalytic language.

What are parents to make of a monster that is their own – that is *them*? 'She is the life we made', as the mother says in the film version of Peter Nichols's *A Day in the Death of Joe Egg*. They love the child because it is their baby; they hate it because it is a travesty of their hopes; they are angry with one another for having failed; they are angry with other people for having let them down ('Look what you have given me', one mother said to the maternity staff); they are depressed because of their own failure; they are guilty because they have let others down and because of their anger; they feel punished because of obscure wrongs they may have done. The power of any one of these feelings is often outside anything they are used to, and the mixture of feelings can be devastating. Small wonder that many parents have thoughts of killing the child. This is not a metaphor, not just a phantasy: it is a real possibility, considered seriously. And for many parents the thought is shocking in the extreme. They have not admitted murderous thoughts before: this time the reality is too near and the thoughts must be repressed, but will not be. Sometimes they only recur in dreams; sometimes they persist for decades; often they are converted into sickness or depression for one or both parents.

Volcanic thoughts like this must be given vent. But often other people conspire, consciously or unconsciously, to repress them. The way in which the news is first broken is an example of this. There are long periods of hesitance or silence among doctors or nurses; the news is announced in places which discourage discussion; supporters are excluded; no time is available. Then, knowing that parents are charged with feeling, but not knowing what, people avoid them: they seem contaminated and dangerous, and social contacts dry up. Is this an exaggeration? Too sensational? One has met well-balanced parents of a happy handicapped child. They do not need social work help. Even they will recognise many of these thoughts. For those who do need help, the picture can be infinitely worse than this. Not all families have two parents: sometimes divorce or death has left the mother alone in her pregnancy, or sometimes she is a teenager for whom the baby anyway means disgrace. Sometimes conception was the result of rape, a marital row or a night with a stranger. Sometimes the child is an 'afterthought' by older parents who already feel foolish about the conception. Sometimes one or other parent has a mentally handicapped brother or sister – married to get away from the situation maybe. Sometimes the parents have just lost a child, had a succession of miscarriages or have other handicapped children. Sometimes their previous children are in care, or the family is burdened by unemployment or debt. The message will be different in every case. Mental handicap has some meanings which are common in our culture, but for each mother and father it has private meanings which can only be drawn out individually. Some people can live with these meanings; for others they are too terrible to contemplate alone. How can these people be helped?

The first point to be made is that it does not matter who gives the help. One mother will see in the face of her midwife that her baby is damaged. She needs help *then* and may get what she needs from the maternity staff. Another will have been told after formal tests have revealed what the eye did not. It may then be possible to choose between a consultant who knows the facts best, a registrar who has time, the GP who knows the family, or a social worker who can follow up afterwards. What counts is that the person who does the telling stays to get the reaction; does it in the right place and with the right people; and comes back often enough to pick up the slow aftermath. It is also important that he or she can give replies, or arrange replies, to the questions that will follow; and that he or she can take a neutral stance on moral issues, clarifying the options but leaving the decision where it belongs.

This particular point is crucial. Killing the child is not a course of action that this society can tolerate. It may nevertheless be important for the parents to look it in the eye. Otherwise they may turn away from forces which could prove too strong later on. It is the job of any counsellor to recognise that thoughts of murder are quite normal for parents in these circumstances; to wait while a painful debate unfolds; to avoid — hardest of all — influencing it one way or another; and then to review the consequences. All too often society's agents rush in to defend their own values. The whole of medicine, and most of nursing, is a denial of death; life is sacred in the law, 'Thou shalt not kill'. It is too disturbing to watch such fundamental values called in question. In short-circuiting the parents' debate with themselves, however, we leave them not knowing their own minds, and not knowing what society would actually do. Many of the resentments which parents of handicapped children still feel years later spring from this root. It is not just that help was not given to care for the child, but that they were never given an open choice. Ideally no parents should be left to look after a child they have not chosen. Society should be prepared to take responsibility for a child who is not chosen. Most parents would still keep their child, but some would be relieved of a lifetime of guilt, and some children could be given love instead of forbearance.

In order to make a proper decision the parents will need a deal of information. Few will know enough about mental handicap to know what its implications are for them; many of the implications will only become clear as the years go by. But the questions flood in. What will he be able to do? What will we have to do for him? What help will we get? What will other people think? What effect will this have on the rest of our family? Many of these are areas for discussion, not for facts, so the process of getting informed is not a simple or a short one. But there is a crucial decision to be made. Some parents say later, 'If I had known then what I know now, I would never have brought him home. I would have smothered him in the hospital. The doctors would have backed me up.' Whether they are right or wrong, they feel they were deceived: they were told there was no choice, that the problems would not be great, that the child was better than he was, or that more help would be available. Or worst of all, they were told nothing. Parents' accounts of this are too consistent to be dismissed. It is clear that many are very poorly supported at this moment of decision and that the difficulty of receiving information under such stress is grossly underestimated. Most will need repeated answers to their questions over several sessions, and this must be on offer.

It is rare that the social worker is left to handle this critical discussion. Far more often it is regarded as a doctor's duty to tell parents that their child is deficient. It may be the obstetrician or a paediatrician — perhaps only a houseman or registrar; it may be the GP; or it may be a psychiatrist who specialises in mental handicap. Perhaps the main task for the social worker is to become aware of who tells and how, and to open up a discussion which can lead to the development of a common policy. It does not have to be the social worker's task to do this: any member of the team might do it; but if there is cause for concern, it is a proper function for the social worker. That sentence could be repeated at many points throughout this book: it describes the essence of overlapping responsibility in multi-disciplinary teams. Good practice is a concern of everyone, whoever actually performs the task in question. If no one else takes it on, there is an obligation on the social worker to do so.

After acceptance

The process of accepting a handicapped child may be a very long one. It is likely to continue long after the child has been brought home. Bayley (1973) suggests that there are five levels of acceptance:

1. a retreat into phantasy, while accepting the child physically;
2. behaving from a sense of duty — an externally imposed obligation;
3. resignation to a bleak fate;
4. acceptance of a personal obligation that one chooses; and
5. love for the child.

Some parents may go through these phases very quickly, or even omit some of them; others may get stuck at any stage. All parents, however, have to create what Bayley calls a 'structure for coping' — a way of dealing with the daily grind of physical care which can be appallingly wearing and depressing. At first, with an infant, this is not radically different for a mentally handicapped child than for any other baby. Sometimes, in fact, mentally handicapped babies are 'very good' babies. The problems of caring may then be mostly emotional and social: they are concerned more with the loss of hopes and the attitudes of others than with the child itself. As the baby gets older, however, and the stigmata of mental handicap become more obvious, the problems gradually enlarge. It is during this phase that parents need practical help above all, and that social workers are judged by their ability to arrange practical means of help. Bayley's research showed that half the parents he interviewed thought their social workers were of little or no help (and these were mental welfare officers before the Seebohm reorganisation), and suggested that their inability to offer the help needed for the daily grind was a major reason for this.

Every aspect of the daily routine may present special difficulty and may require an inordinate amount of time. Sleep patterns may be disturbed, with fits and nightmares or just early waking; strange noises may disturb others; incontinence may be routine. Waking may be irregular, so that other routines may be interrupted. Dressing and bathing, feeding, dealing with incontinence, may all present extra problems. Individual children produce their own patterns of complication and there can be no general rules about what causes greatest exasperation or what is most helpful. For instance, one little girl born with deformations of her hips has to be lifted every-where: into the bath, out of it, into bed and out of it, from her chair to her potty, up to the table, on to the floor to play and so on. This adds enormously to the physical burden of her care and means that she needs attention almost constantly so that she does not damage her joints by keeping them in one position too long or by using them too much. It also means that the whole pattern of her occupation has to be specially designed: she cannot be left to play, quickly gets frustrated when things are out of her reach, needs special adaptations for some of her playthings, a special seat for the car, special clothing and so on. And all this is additional to the problems of mental handicap!

For a child such as this parents are likely to need support from several people with special skills: paediatrician and orthopaedic surgeon, physiotherapist and occupational thera-pist, aids technician and psychologist. And the help required will be of a detailed kind, not easily reduced to textbook advice. Much of it could only be offered by an expert who had watched the daily routines at home, to spot the child's peculiar needs – and the parents' peculiar responses. Did you know that a child who will resist all attempts to open a clenched fist by force will immediately release it if the hand is turned palm downwards and gentle pressure is applied to the knuckles? Nor did her parents until they had struggled with the problem of washing her for years! This kind of technical knowledge can make a vast difference to the pleasure of bath-time and alter the whole experience for the parents. Similar kinds of advice are needed about feeding, sleeping arrangements, dressing and all the other activities of daily life. And they change with time, as the child's muscles develop or his weight becomes more than the mother can handle, or it becomes necessary to teach new skills. Many parents have said that the best help they got with such problems came from other parents: either in the form of discussion with more experienced parents or in the form of written material from specialist voluntary organisations. The Down's Children's Association in particular has an excellent reputation for giving parents just the kind of practical information that they most need.

Then there is the whole problem of difficult behaviour. Mentally handicapped children find all manner of devices for annoying their parents, consciously or inadvertently. They spit and they dangle bits of string; they rock and bang their heads; they hum, sing or tap on walls. Most of these habits start from some stimulus which they have found satisfying and which had a function for them. Sometimes they may continue to have some developmental function. Often they are begun because they attract attention from parents and instead of being discouraged they are reinforced. Most parents unravel tangles like these in due course, but there are times when even the most competent could use the help of a good, practical behavioural psychologist. And most would have a much easier time if some external observer, whom they could trust, came regularly enough to see such processes in embryo.

There are three levels of help which parents need at different stages with problems of behaviour. The first is witness. Elizabeth Irvine, provoked by social workers' records which only said 'Saw Mrs Brown today', once wrote scathingly about 'see therapy'. But actually there is a function in witnessing. Mannoni (1973) puts this point explicitly when she describes parents who, although they accept the diagnosis the doctors have attached to their child, continue to seek further opinions or ask for treatment. It is not, she suggests, that they really hope for anything different, but that they need someone to recognise the burden they are carrying; to see their own strain and the damage their child has borne; to avoid being trapped in their own phantasies. In a sense anyone can provide this witness, but it is of limited value because it leads nowhere.

The second level is defusing and refocusing; interrupting a recurrent pattern of behaviour and helping to establish new patterns. This is the kind of help that a sensitive neighbour, who knows the situation well, can offer. It involves seeing enough of the interchanges to guess why they take the form they do, and being willing to make an honest comment, at the risk of offending. Few people have such neighbours, however. Most rarely get beyond 'Why don't you . . .?' or 'Have you tried . . .?' They are not well enough informed about what the family has been through and diffident about their ability to come up with anything new. A good deal of social work interviewing falls into a similar pattern. It is infuriating, and professionally incompetent, because it conveys that the social worker is only half-interested and not serious about finding a solution. The social worker should aim, as a minimum, at providing honest comment on what he or she sees happening, staying long enough to see what is happening and long enough to get the full reaction to the comment.

The third level of help is efficient training or therapy. Most behavioural problems can be tackled by retraining, once they have been fully understood. This includes the retraining of the parents and their co-operation in looking at their own behaviour is essential. Social workers should by now be familiar with the theory of conditioning, with the use of rewards to alter behaviour and the idea that subtle rewards are offered between parent and child without either being aware of them. The effectiveness of this way of thinking about ordinary problems of daily life has been demonstrated so often that it has become an essential tool for helping the parents of mentally handicapped children. This does not necessarily mean that social workers have to be experts in behaviourist therapy themselves. If they work with psychologists or others who are skilled at this kind of training, they may be able to draw them freely into collaborative work. If not, there is a strong argument for their seeking training, or at least consultation in behaviourist methods of task analysis, so that they can have some real impact on practical problems in the home. There are useful accounts of behaviourist methods in Perkins (1971), Poteet (1974) and Carr (1980), which are designed to give practical help to parents.

The problems are by no means only in the mentally handicapped child. In coming to terms with their child, parents may react in innumerable ways, some of them neurotic and destructive. Some parents have had personal difficulties from childhood, which are merely refocused by the arrival of a damaged child.

*   *   *

Mrs Peters always felt put down by her own mother, who compared her unfavourably with her younger sister. Marriage meant a relief from this demoralising atmosphere: it was something she had created which was good, although her mother was usually able to find fault. When her first child turned out to be mentally handicapped, all her worst fears about herself seemed to be confirmed and she became very depressed.

*   *   *

Sometimes the parents' marriage has been in difficulties from the start, and the mentally handicapped child merely provides a fresh burden to test it.

*   *   *

Mr and Mrs Preston married young and had a stormy first year or two. Mrs Preston twice left her husband and stayed with friends, because she could not stand the arguments any longer. After the second episode, they agreed to start a family in the hope that a child would unite them. When the child was found to be mentally handicapped they were completely thrown, and blamed one another. They tried to have the child taken into hospital care but were told this was not necessary. Mrs Preston fell ill a month after the birth, and as soon as she was better her husband left home. Guilt has brought him back twice since then, but mutual recriminations soon poison the atmosphere and the marriage is clearly very unstable.

*   *   *

In cases like these the mentally handicapped child merely fits into a drama that has been going on for some time. Obviously he or she may greatly accentuate the drama, but does not hold the centre of the stage. Yet many forces conspire to put him or her into that position. Scapegoats are always welcome as an explanation for failure, and other people regard mental handicap with such awe that it is often quite hard for parents to avoid coming to believe that the child is the root of all their problems. Sometimes they are themselves conscious of the false position their child has been put into, and even jealous of the attention that he or she attracts. 'I wish people would sometimes ask how I am, or help me to learn something new.'

Sometimes, the child does seem to bring to the surface difficulties that were not visible before. Sometimes one parent has much greater difficulty than the other in accepting the child and may gradually cut him- or herself off from the family, retreating perhaps into excessive overtime or nightwork, or merely arranging the day so that there is no opportunity for talking. Sometimes one parent becomes identified with the handicapped child to the exclusion of other children, and the other parent may attempt to redress the balance, falling into conflict as a result. In cases like these the handicapped child plays an important part in the family drama, and is the fulcrum around which much of the action takes place. The sources of tension lie perhaps deep in the personalities of the parents, but a major crisis was required, such as the birth of a handicapped child, to evoke clear signs of it.

One cannot repeat too often that the problem must not be assumed to be mental handicap. When anxiety is running high it is not always the obvious source of complaint which creates the drama: the really painful issues are often secret ones which are masked by those that can be made explicit. Acute anxiety, which seems to be about the mentally handicapped member of the family but does not subside whatever action is taken, may well attach to a quite different issue – to a suspected illness that has not yet been diagnosed, to a sexual affair that has not yet been challenged, or to criminal behaviour by a teenager which has not yet been confronted. It is important, as in all casework, to be sensitive to feelings which are too strong for their apparent source.

It is equally important to balance this by saying that not all parents of a mentally handicapped child have neurotic problems. Most suffer grossly from inadequate support of quite ordinary kinds, and it is the first responsibility of society to give them the tools they need to do their job: nurseries, day care, short-term residential care, hostels, good local schools, and advice and information. If these services were widely available it might be much easier to see which families needed more personal help as well.

Parents talk scathingly about the incompetence of social

workers during this part of their lives. 'She was a nice girl, but did not know anything about mental handicap. She did not pretend to. I had to tell her everything. I don't mind training social workers, but it is not much help to us.' What is needed in the early stages is a guide to what can be expected: parents have a right to be warned, by someone who has experience, of the pitfalls that await them. Later, when they have found them, they have a right to be told how others have coped; what options exist; what resources can be offered; and what they will have to do themselves.

They also have a right to have services provided in a simple and straightforward way. So often the social worker has to engage in complicated negotiations to obtain the smallest service: a home help for a couple of hours a week; payment for day nursery attendance; short-term care for a week in the summer. In the present climate of service cuts, these are likely to become even more discretionary — even more at the whim of managers who are detached from the clients. This is not a problem that the social worker can tackle single-handed. If resources are inadequate then there will always be some form of rationing. The political task of winning more resources is one that professionals can engage in, but they must do so corporately. It is also possible for social workers, singly or corporately, to insist on knowing what criteria are to be used for rationing. This makes it harder to adjust the system for hard cases, but far easier for social workers to predict the outcome of an application. The important point here is that parents need to know, well in advance, what help they can expect. If they are building an effective routine for themselves, as they need to, they must be able to see the relief points and work towards them.

These relief points are what Bayley (1973) calls the 'structure for living', as compared with the 'structure for coping': they introduce some quality into a life that threatens to be mere survival. For a variety of reasons parents get caught in a seemingly unbroken cycle of toil. Some have not had a holiday together for many years; some never go anywhere at the weekends, never get out in the evening. The cycle is familiar for anyone who has worked with single parents or the depressed mothers of pre-school children. The daily grind is so heavy that in the evening or at the weekend one has not the energy to go out; has not had the foresight to book tickets, arrange baby-sitters or transport; and anyway has lost the belief in one-self as an out-going adult. The problems of explaining family routines to a stranger seem daunting, and the peculiarities of one's child so humiliating that outside help is not acceptable. Identification with the child has become so strong that to leave him or her is physically painful, emotionally exhausting. If society seems to confirm that parents are not entitled to help through short-term relief or domiciliary care, then the cycle is confirmed: people get the message that they are demanding and ineligible, and do not seek help after the first few rebuffs.

It is of the greatest possible help in such situations for parents to meet others who have been through this cycle and know what it feels like. There are some, who have not accepted that their child is handicapped, perhaps, for whom this is not acceptable. But most can believe that fellow sufferers understand; can listen to their warnings more readily; can accept their advice; and get a truer sense of their rights and better relief of their guilt than from professionals, how-ever sensitive. In many areas effective parents' groups now exist. The National Society for Mentally Handicapped Children and Parents alone has some 400 parents' groups. They vary in what they can undertake: some employ their own welfare worker; others have welfare visitors who are volunteers from their own membership; some run nursery groups or baby-sitting schemes; some are principally campaigning organis-ations who bring pressure to bear on statutory organisations. Social workers have often been slow to collaborate with these groups, finding themselves on the sharp end of criticism too often for comfort. But they are an enormously valuable resource, and a sensitive forum, for social workers to use when they come across insoluble problems. Where a group does not exist, it may well be the first job of social workers to help to set one up. They may become a rod for the back of officialdom, but only if officialdom is too wedded to the status quo.

One of the most effective parents' organisations is to be found in Southend, where since 1970 Dr M. Mellor has gradually helped to develop a variety of self-help operations. These began with a group of six couples who met on sixteen occasions for three to four hours, talking their way from anger to information, and through an educational programme to preparation for leadership. Members of this group then started two more groups for other parents, who went through a similar process, and in turn started two more groups, for parents of children in different age groups (0–2 and 2–8). The first of these ran for many years, expanded to thirty or forty members at times, attracted people from thirty miles away and eventually hived off two more groups – for parents in one particular locality and for parents whose children had moved on to school. The groups sometimes meet together to hear guest speakers. The members offer expert advice to one another, and can visit the parents of a new mentally handicapped child within a day or so of the diagnosis. Further groups developed for the 2–8-year-old group: one was for parents of multiply handicapped children; another, interestingly, for parents of children under observation at the children's day centre for developmental problems. A training programme was developed for professionals and parents on sex education and the mentally handicapped; and two further groups for parents of children aged 8 to 12 and of teenagers. Summing up this experience after seven years, Dr Mellor commented:

> We find that the families gain definite benefit, they are less isolated, develop dignity, are less frustrated, develop purpose, receive companionship and support, gain information and help in self-understanding and family relationships, learn how to develop their children, learn of stages of child development, and above all impart help and information not otherwise received from or available from professionals. We now have a new type of family, in which the aggression associated with the tragedy of a handicapped child has disappeared and been replaced with hope, insight and activity.

Parent support groups of a similar kind have been tried elsewhere with similar success; and it is clear that they provide an excellent way of garnering the painfully won experience of parents, and of keeping morale high by a communal approach.

Facing out

The outside world does otherwise represent a considerable threat to parents of a handicapped child. From the start they have had to face it in the shape of doctors or nurses, if the child's handicap was noticed at birth, or in the shape of those who have been involved in establishing the nature of developmental problems. But in a sense these professionals are in the conspiracy: they understand about these things and could see what was coming. It is quite different with relatives and friends. In the event of a birth, they have known the baby was due and have to be told the news. Some of them are drawn into support, but one of the first disturbing facts is that others withdraw. Some people seem to experience the handicapped child itself as an affront or an insult: they are shocked and can only reject the experience. Others are thrown into embarrassment and confusion, and deal with this by withdrawal — from the disaster area as it were. They may not wish to do so, but in waiting for an initiative from the parents they seem to convey that they are stand-offish and perhaps disgusted. Talking about their friends, parents have indicated that the people who are most help are those who can behave normally; pick up the baby and find out what he or she can do; talk about things of an everyday kind; do not have to express pity or sorrow. There is a tendency anyway to feel that a great gulf has opened between life before the disaster and life after it, and anything which helps to bridge this gulf is welcome.

Unless help of this kind has been around, there is likely to be a period when a small in-group develops — of those who are in the secret — and the family becomes very in-turned. Then the first steps back into contact with the outside world may be acutely difficult and painful. Taking the baby out means showing him off. Neighbours who would normally expect to come and congratulate may be faced with sudden embarrassment, crossing the street to avoid it or having their congratulations interrupted by sudden realisation of what has happened. People are not trained to cope with this situation and react in sometimes unbelievable ways. Hannam (1975) quotes one as saying, 'You wouldn't have wanted a genius, would you?'; another as saying, 'He'll never leave you.' It is all too easy for the parents to overreact to these stupidities and turn back in on themselves; to get a reputation for becoming difficult and strange, and gradually to lose contact with neighbours and friends again. Then every small commerce of daily life can become very stressful — shopping, going to the doctor, going to church — and there is a temptation to reject invitations.

As time goes on, these things fall into a pattern. The situation is known, and neighbours have worked out ways of avoiding contact or of limiting it. Or, one must thankfully recognise, friendships have been strengthened which make it possible for social life to continue. There may still be difficulties and even shocks. As children grow older their ways are better known, but they may still be acutely embarrassing in public, upsetting displays in shops, making peculiar gestures and approaching people inappropriately, coping badly with traffic and so on. Some of these adventures lead to abuse from startled strangers, and mothers have often been reduced to tears by the behaviour or remarks of passers-by. 'How can they let them swim in the same water!' 'It ought not to be allowed, startling other children like that.' 'Ought to be put away.' And worse!

Even in the area where they are known there may be tensions and embarrassment. Some mentally handicapped children are great wanderers and will enter other people's houses or gardens with no compunction. If neighbours are unsympathetic this can cause enormous tension because the child has to be watched every minute of the day. Even by standing and staring or by following other children, the mentally handicapped child can upset neighbours. These contretemps mark the time when parents begin to come to terms with the ways in which society deals with anomaly.

An additional problem which can arise when neighbours are anxious to be helpful is denial of the problem. If they get over the first hurdles, sustain their relationship and relate directly to the child, they sometimes fall into false reassurance (to themselves as much as anyone): 'Isn't she doing marvellously', 'He seems so bright', 'Goodness what a charmer!' To a mother who is only just keeping depression at bay this can

be devastating. It removes any excuse for her own bad feelings and makes it impossible for her to admit to them. Professionals and even other parents are also liable to fall into
this trap. One local society became so accustomed to taking
new parents of a handicapped child to see Mrs X, 'who has
managed wonderfully for ten years' that Mrs X could not
escape her role as paragon to ask for help herself and eventually
broke down. There is a delicate balance between defensive
withdrawal by neighbours and cheery intrusiveness which
ignores the depression.

Perhaps this is the place to mention a general problem for
parents and social workers — ambivalence about help. Little
enough help is available. Often, though, parents find it
exceedingly hard to accept help when it is offered. This can
happen with any kind of help, but it is especially likely when
the help involves handing over the care of the child to a
stranger or strangers. When first offered a place in a hostel or
hospital for short-term care, for instance, some parents panic
and turn the offer down; or allow the child to go but then
retrieve him or her. There are rational reasons for this: the
child will be (or is indeed found to be) unsettled; people will
not know his or her routines or communications; it is hard to
explain to the child what is happening. But another factor is
often present as well. This becomes clear when, as sometimes
happens, the parents start to ask for more care, and then full-
time care, and then seem to lose interest in the child. It is as
if the initial resistance was from fear of starting on a slippery
slope which could only lead to rejection. Perhaps total responsibility is easier to accept than partial. It does certainly seem
that the emotional attachment of the parents to their child is
sometimes very strong — it has to be for the child to survive
at all — and that the prospect of involving other people in his
or her care produces strange ambivalence. This is compounded
of fear that others will be able to do better than they can;
anxiety that their peculiar ways of coping with the child, and
their failures, will become public knowledge; and panic that
if they begin to have hope for themselves again — hope of a
free life — they will let a genie out of a bottle, which they
will never be able to replace. Feelings of this kind are by no
means unknown to parents of any child who has to go into

hospital, but for parents of a handicapped child they may be very intense, especially if the first feelings of anger and rebellion at having the child have not been resolved.

As a way of easing these 'all-or-nothing' attitudes, the value of day care at an early stage cannot be overestimated. At one level it gives the parents, especially the mother, a break, and provides a space for practical tasks or merely recovery. On another level it provides the child with different sorts of stimulus, vents energy, breaks patterns of provocation and irritation, introduces the child to other children if there are no siblings, and provides an opportunity for some specific training. If the mother can be involved herself, it may also be possible to show her ways of teaching and training that she has not thought of for herself.

For the first aim, day care can be provided by almost any-one: a friend who will take over in her own home is just as effective as a professional. People are extraordinarily reluctant to place burdens on their friends, or even to allow it to be seen that they have needs. It is often useful, therefore, for an outsider to provide the excuse for such a demand to be made, and even to make the first contacts. There is the special sense of shame and anxiety which comes from having a child who is damaged, and perhaps unpredictable in his or her behaviour. One does not want to risk losing one's friends, who may be few in number; and even to see one's child through someone else's eyes can be very disturbing. However, it is important to take these risks, if at all possible. Other people introduce a note of reality to a world which can be very encapsulated; and the fact of the relationship surviving can be very reassur-ing: 'He can't be so bad after all.'

Sometimes it seems easier for parents to cope with their own feelings if they are caught up in a web of relationships in which obligations are diffused. Increasingly playgroups are showing themselves willing to take one or two handicapped children, and find that they are contained relatively easily. Groups which have not thought of this might be helped to consider the idea, and playgroup advisers of local authority SSDs might be encouraged to take up the theme. In some areas also the 'opportunity group' has provided the answer for a small number of handicapped children. Meeting perhaps once a week in a primary school hall, such a group can be a valuable respite for parents, and a focus for voluntary work by, for example, children from the local secondary school. If experienced professionals are available, an opportunity group can be far more than this: a good preparation for schooling, and a platform for the development of teaching methods for handicapped children. Finally, one must include the more obvious nursery school placement. Apart from parental anxiety, one of the barriers to the effective use of nursery school placements is the diffidence of ordinary nursery teachers to deal with the mentally handicapped. One or two special schools have therefore devised an extension of the Portage Scheme (M. and D. Shearer, 1972) and are making their staff available to those in nursery and infant schools, to teach techniques for working with mentally handicapped children. These have in practice proved valuable for a much wider group of children who have learning difficulties, and the benefits of the scheme have been unexpectedly great.

Short-term care has already been mentioned and this is a vitally important resource for many families. There seems to be a shift of responsibility taking place at present, and many local authorities are at last providing short-term care for mentally handicapped children who have previously been accepted only in hospitals. The ways in which this is being done vary around the country: some authorities have built special hostels; some have set aside places in children's community homes; some use residential facilities at special schools during school holidays or at weekends; some take over buildings for periods during the summer. Maureen Oswin has been studying these different methods and she points out that in many areas the provision is very inflexible, giving good reason for parental misgivings. She suggests that there is too general an assumption that mentally handicapped children are a burden which must be lifted at all costs, that parents are only anxious to get their own freedom, and that the children are insensitive to the way in which their care is organised. She points out that when care is arranged in a hostel serving a large area, children are often transported to it in an impersonal way, and only their escorts on the journey see their anxiety and confusion. At the hostel, disturbed behaviour is attributed to their mental handicap, and not to separation as it would be with ordinary children. Often the staff change from one period of care to another, and from shift to shift, so that there can be little continuity of interest or relationship, and the many small cues, in words and behaviour, which make real communication possible are not transmitted from home to their carers. If mentally handicapped children were treated like other children, more attention would be paid to their feelings – to selecting a type of holiday for them which made them most at home, and to building in continuities with their home life. Sending them away with ordinary children's organisations might seem to be a better option for older children, and more use would be made of arrangements like fostering on a very local level. Where special efforts have been made to find, train and give appropriate remuneration to holiday hosts, parents have found themselves much better satisfied with the short-term care arrangements, although they have encountered new anxieties: 'I keep worrying that our John will be too much for Mrs Williams: it works so well that I am afraid it will all vanish.' Such local arrangements can offer not only one or two longer holidays each year, but day or weekend opportunities; and in fact often turn into family friendships. From the planners' point of view they avoid the need for capital investment, and there seems to be every indication that they can deal with children, and indeed adults, of every level of disability – provided that sufficient effort is put into finding suitable hosts, and into preparing the relationship between them and the families of the mentally handicapped children. A preliminary version of Maureen Oswin's report is available in the form of a discussion paper from the Kings Fund Centre (Oswin 1981).

One scheme, developed in Toronto, which bears directly on the issue of short-term care although it has a wider supportive function, is 'Extend a Family'. This was created by a group of parents who set out to find host families who would undertake to provide not more than thirty days' supportive care a year – whether for a few hours at a time or for longer holiday periods. Hosts are carefully matched with the families they help, and the scheme is kept local so that relationships can grow through easy contact. This is very much the basis on which Maureen Oswin suggests short-term care might be developed.

The school intervenes

If all the earlier problems have been adequately dealt with, school may be welcomed whole-heartedly by the parents of a mentally handicapped child. It represents a huge relief in terms of removal of the burden of hour-by-hour care. The same is true for children who are not mentally handicapped. Special problems arise, however, with mentally handicapped children, and the ambivalences which often mark the transition for any parent are especially marked for those with a handicapped child.

In the first place, the handicap may not yet have been accepted. It may indeed only emerge as the question of school placement is faced. Parents whose hopes are still based on a change of diagnosis may be very unwilling to accept placement in a special school or special class. Whether special education offers advantages is a very topical issue and some parents will be involved in the battle for integration. Some education authorities, on the other hand, may be strongly in favour of special education and there is room for considerable conflict at this point. Parents are advised to talk with others who have older children, and have experience of the particular schools and classes in the area. The issue is not one to be resolved ideologically. Good education can be offered in either a special setting or an ordinary setting, and it depends on the commitment of the teachers and the structure of the school whether it is in fact delivered.

Even when the school has been agreed, however, tensions remain. The school may represent the first major opportunity for the parents to see their child in the hands of the state; judged by professionals; set to achieve goals they have not selected. The child is on trial, and so in a real sense are they. 'Are the other children better or worse?' 'Will the child be too much for the teachers?' 'Can the school do better than us? They ought to be able to, but how can they know him as well as we do?' It is the first time that all the child's quirks have been exposed throughout the day to other people, and that all the eccentric ways the parents have developed for coping have been shown to others who have standards.

New practical problems are likely to emerge. Getting the child awake, dressed and fed before the school transport arrives becomes a new kind of nightmare. The pressure may make it harder to achieve, as the child becomes resistant. The transport itself may be unreliable, arriving early or after the child has been ready for an hour (and has just wet himself again). It may be necessary to supply several sets of clothing (all perfect of course) if the child is incontinent. The evenings may become more difficult if the child is exhausted by the day, by new experiences and by travelling. There is the constant worry about how it is going. A whole new routine has to emerge, which in the early stages at least may take much of the shine off the relief that is also felt.

Much depends on how the parents and school are able to relate to one another. Some schools are very sensitive to the problems of new parents and go to great lengths to learn their fears and achievements before they receive the child. Some are excellent at telling parents what their child is doing, sending work home, exchanging information daily through a home/school diary in which important events are recorded, and attempting to create an integrated learning process between home and school. Some parents are well able to handle the school staff, and ensure that their views are known and the child's growth points are identified. But this is not always so. Some schools are quite blind to the role parents play and treat them as if they were an awkward interference with the learning process. Some parents doubt the ability of the school to understand their child and treat the staff with suspicion; or have a dislike of teachers which goes back to their own schooldays; or are still smarting from their encounter with the education office in the discussion about placement.

The social worker's role in all this may be very difficult, especially if he or she has doubts about the schooling that is available. Whatever kind of job the social worker has, there are some general guidelines about such difficulties. First, the laws relating to mentally handicapped people are the same as

those for any school age child. The education authority
has a duty to provide education suited to the child's needs
and the child must attend school. The parents have a right to
express their choice about the kind of education the child
should receive, but cannot insist on attendance at a particular
school. Second, the overall aim is to arrange for the child to
be helped to develop as a whole human being, as fast and as
completely as possible. There is room for debate about how
this should be achieved: debate about the educational objectives at any one time; about the teaching methods; and about
the social context of the school – its human relationships
and facilities. It will help if both parents and school can say
as clearly as possible what they think should be achieved and
how. Sometimes this kind of openness can clear the air
enough for agreement to emerge. Sometimes, however, major
ideological or methodological differences exist, and the social
worker may be caught between them. Then the specific job
that the social worker has will influence the way in which he
or she can behave. Rather than discuss this in the abstract, I
would like to look at two contrasted situations of conflict
which were resolved in quite different ways.

*   *   *

In the first situation, the social worker was employed by the parents
themselves as a welfare visitor. She therefore had no loyalty to the local
authority as such. In the course of her visits she got the impression that
some parents were very dissatisfied that the centralised special school
involved far too much travelling and separation of their children from
the ordinary life of the communities they lived in, and they were not
convinced that this was justified by the school's having adopted the
most recent and effective methods of educating their pupils. The parents'
organisation convened a meeting of the dissatisfied parents to find out
what common ground they had, and what common goals they could
subscribe to. This led to several months' study of what actually existed,
of the attitudes teachers and education officials had, and of the legis-
lation. The social worker was asked to recommend a course of action
but declined, feeling that it was essential for those who would do the
fighting to choose their own battleground. They began 'reasonable
discussions' with the education officials, but felt these became very
defensive and inflexible. They then became more aggressive and used
publicity to ventilate their case. The local authority remained immobile,

and as a result of the publicity a private school offered to experiment with the inclusion of some mentally handicapped children in its classes. This was by no means what the parents or the social worker had expected, or wanted, but has emerged as a partial solution to their demand for integrated education, and a demonstration of what can be done.

*   *   *

In the second situation, a local authority social worker based in a hospital, found the parents in one family very unhappy about the allocation of their son to a special school several miles from their home. They were convinced that the school would not meet his needs and refused to send him. The social worker shared some of these doubts, feeling apprehensive about the effect of two long journeys each day but, more importantly, feeling that the school was not providing the kind of individual stimulus that the children required. There were no special classes in ordinary schools in the area and private education was beyond the parents' means. The social worker therefore helped to arrange a meeting between the parents and the deputy head of the school. At first this was unpromising: the parents presented their anxieties about the school baldly and the deputy head reacted defensively. But when the parents talked about the sleeping difficulties that had been making life very hard for them, the teacher found something that she could relate to and described how another family had coped with similar problems. The social worker got the teacher to talk about the pressure on staff in the school and she was able to hint at disagreements among the staff. Suddenly the situation seemed human again and the parents' anxiety about the journey could be tackled directly. They agreed on a two-week trial, during which the father would bring the child to school each morning but he would be returned by bus in the afternoon. At the end of this period, the parents remained critical of certain aspects of the school's routine, but could also see that gains had been made. They undertook to put their weight into the parent–teacher association, and have been very active in organising a programme of volunteers to help with speech training.

*   *   *

These two approaches are not in conflict with one another. The social worker in each case could not claim credit alone for the resolution of the problem. In each case certain elements of the original problem were not resolved anyway: in the first case, a new form of segregation had been achieved, although in an integrated school; in the second, the parents had had to accommodate themselves, very largely, to an unsatisfactory school. The first social worker, however, free of the constraints of being part of a large organisation with a complicated alliance with the education system and, more significantly, having a primary loyalty to the parents' wishes, was able to help the parents discover strength and independence. Whether the final solution was better than in the second case remains arguable, but the parents felt more powerful. In the second case, the social worker was more directly involved in the negotiations and was able to play a more direct role in choosing the outcome — the role is perhaps more familiar for caseworkers — but it seems likely that the parents were left with some feeling of having been manipulated out of their anger.

One should not exaggerate these problems. Since 1971 there has been such a positive change in the education of mentally handicapped school children that most parents find they have a predominantly good experience with their child's school, and the staff of many special schools are sensitive to the parental and other social dimensions of their work. Social workers are likely to find ready allies in the staffroom, if they are prepared to invest a little time in making themselves known; and this can be a rich source of consultation and advice on learning methods. The social worker can often provide a reciprocal service by explaining some of the mysteries of community services or of family reactions, to school staff; and, as in other settings, it is very helpful to be well known when problems arise.

Because of the nature of their work social workers often appear to be identified with the most difficult children, or the most difficult parents, from the point of view of the school. They are often involved in pressing the school to change their rules or make exceptions, to tolerate disruption or confusion, or to go on trying with someone they are tempted to reject (child or parent again!). Whether the issue is school attendance or school leaving, misbehaviour on the bus or in the playground, or demands by parents about their child's progress, the social worker can often act as a valuable catalyst — if he or she is well enough known to both parties.

Probably the area of greatest misunderstanding during the school years is the establishment of common aims for the child. Estimates of ability are likely to vary dramatically from professional to professional, and it is not surprising that parents are often out of touch with the school, or vice versa. Sometimes parents are critical of low achievement, as they see it, at school; sometimes they find it hard to believe that their child is capable of what the school says he or she can do. This is partly a product of changing beliefs in education; and partly a product of the fluid hopes and fears that public attitudes to mental handicap engender. Unless the school has done a very good job of facilitating communication with parents through the early years of schooling, these tensions are likely to increase as a child moves into his or her last few years at school. It becomes increasingly important for parents that their child can read or write, if at all possible, and has developed social and practical skills that will give him or her the best chance of an independent life, or at least of a productive adulthood. On the other hand, the idea of greater independence — with the implication that more risks must be taken — can be quite threatening to parents who have been very protective through childhood. Education is about personal development, and risk-taking is not only inevitable but essential. For those parents who have taken their duty to care most seriously, there may be a real problem as the school tries to widen horizons; and they may unconsciously undermine these efforts. A good school will be well aware of the need to negotiate about this, and to use public meetings and private interviews, and invoke the help of other parents in accommodating such attitudes. Quite often social workers will find themselves in similar issues — over short-term care, or other ways of bringing relief to parents and opportunity to their children — and it will be useful to everyone if the issues can be brought out into the open in some kind of review. Although the education of the child is central to all work with his or her family, it should not be assumed that the school has a monopoly of skill in identifying his or her needs. The ability and disability of each child, and the pattern of life in each family produces an individual constellation of needs, and there will be times when the school needs help to refocus its work with a particular child. Social workers can sometimes help parents to call for a review that achieves this refocusing, and should aim to put themselves into a relationship with the school that makes it possible to do this without undue threat.

School leaving: where next?

School leaving brings to a head a number of questions which have been growingly insistent as childhood has rolled on. The school will have been a constant feature of life for eleven years or more. For some mentally handicapped people there is no doubt that they have come to feel frustrated in it. They know that their brothers or sisters, perhaps, or friends from home, have moved on to jobs in the adult world, and they feel restricted by an environment which is largely designed for younger children. For another group, however, leaving school means the loss of important continuities, and uncertainty about what is to follow can produce behaviour problems.

For parents, similar issues may arise. For one family whose child has seemed rather 'stuck' during the last year of schooling, the move to a more adult setting may seem healthy and desirable. For another, it may mean only the loss of trusted teachers who have understood the particular problems of the family, and a doubtful future with new helpers.

At this point the social worker may come into a new prominence as controller of the key resource — the ATC. Different local authorities manage this second allocation crisis in different ways. In some the decision is left to negotiation between the school head and the ATC manager; in others, where places in the ATC are in short supply, the allocation may be made in the divisional office. In some the pupils are transferred together, at a formal date; in others the move is made according to individual need and state of preparedness, at any time in the school year.

The social worker may have an even more important role if no place is available in the ATC. Some families are thrown into complete disarray if it suddenly becomes clear that their mentally handicapped teenage son or daughter is going to be at home all day. This can mean that one parent has to give up work, that new stresses fall on the marriage, that relationships with neighbours may be jeopardised. Ironically, the people most likely to be affected are the most handicapped, or those whose behaviour is most difficult; the most needy, one might think. Sometimes — equally ironically — a more able youngster may be caught out, because he or she wants a job, not a training placement, or because his or her parents do not favour the ATC.

Further education is one of the areas in which recent developments have been most beneficial, but there is a long way to go for some authorities. Problems may come to the social worker which are not individual problems at all, but need to be tackled at the level of social action. What are the principles involved? The fundamental point is that at the age of 16 all mentally handicapped people are still in a phase of active development and learning. They have started later, and moved more slowly than the average child; they have a long way to go still; and many are learning more actively in their mid-teens than ever before. Their maturation will go on until the mid-20s anyway, and it is perfectly clear that they should be entitled to several years of further education. To put the same point another way: they are likely to repay an invest-ment in their education with greatly enhanced independence in their later years.

The only serious argument against making this an edu-cational responsibility is the economic one. Adult training centres usually have a staff ratio half as favourable as special schools. If local education departments were responsible for the further education of the mentally handicapped, whether in ATCs, further education colleges or in some other setting, they would insist on higher staffing ratios, as they did when they took over the junior training centres in 1971, and probably — in the long term — on longer training for staff than is now available. It is no doubt heresy to say so, but I believe that in so far as ATCs are educational establishments they should be managed by local education authorities and not by social services departments, because this is the normal pattern and puts the emphasis squarely on learning. In the foreseeable future this seems an unlikely move, and social workers will usually be dealing with their own management when problems arise.

As suggested earlier, these problems are likely to concern

individuals who cannot be contained within the ATCs, or who do not believe their needs will be met there. Serious gaps do still exist in many areas. In particular there is often a significant gap between the day care provided by mental handicap hospitals and that provided by ATCs. It makes no sense, but hospitals do often reject quite handicapped people on the grounds that they are not handicapped enough for their services, while ATCs maintain that they are too handicapped for the centre programme. This kind of boundary dispute will always arise when resources are short and there is a need for rationing, and when the co-ordinating machinery for joint planning is ineffectual. The problem can only be tackled by planning means – ensuring that there is no gap between services, or establishing an intermediary service in the gap. The social worker caught in the middle may be able to prise a door open for one client, or two; but should never accept that the issue is only a casework one. If a teenager who has educational needs is trapped without teaching, this is so clearly evidence of an insufficiently caring community that the message must go back to the policy-makers. Alongside whatever attempts are being made to place the individual, therefore, there must be parallel efforts to demonstrate the existence of a gap, to work out an effective way of filling it and to campaign for resources to do so. This will routinely involve putting pressure on senior staff, if they exist, and using whatever interdisciplinary forums there may be to review the problem. But it may also involve recruiting parents' support, and helping them to develop a campaign strategy. The problems this can cause for social workers will be discussed further in Chapter 6.

This transition period is of great importance for parents. They have often asked themselves what place their child can occupy in society, and this is a crucial opportunity to test phantasy against reality – as it is for any parent. It is also a time when the willingness of society to tolerate, care for and use their child is put to the test. And if they have not already started to consider the question, 'What happens when we have gone?', they begin to see this issue emerging clearly.

The meaning of mental handicap comes out more clearly again for the parents at this time. They have come through the previous ten or eleven years with more or less pain and difficulty, but most have established a pattern of trust, or at least familiar hostility, with school or hospital staff. They know that the peculiarities of their child, and their own faults and foibles have been understood and tolerated. They have known how to make the system work for them. Now this is to be changed and they will have to face, first, a period of indecision until it is clear what kind of placement can be offered, and then a period of testing out new relationships and of resolving new problems. All this may be easier for a child who is in hospital, where the shifts occur within an overall structure and it is clear who is making the decisions. For a child who is at home, the parents may only be half-involved in the decision process, and may experience a great deal of uncertainty and anxiety as the crisis approaches.

There are problems which coincide with school leaving, but are not related to it. Often an approach to the social worker in the last year of schooling about a housing problem or about holiday arrangements is an attempt to open up anxieties about future placement, or dissatisfaction with the level a child has reached in school. Sometimes, though, the other problems are real enough and may, conversely, be causing difficulty for the child.

*   *   *

Brian's father was obliged to change his job at the same time as Brian was due to leave school and the family had to plan to move house. Brian had already visited the ATC and was apparently looking forward to his own move, but became morose and difficult in school when he learned his father's news. This was very puzzling to the school staff; and it came to a head when Brian ran away from school one day, tried to walk home and was picked up by the police for nearly causing an accident. The school asked the social worker to try and find out what was going on at home, and only then did news of their impending move get through to the school.

*   *   *

One might wish that the parents and the school had been in closer touch with one another, or feel that the parents, in particular, were at fault in not reporting their change of plan. But such failures are the product of the relationship that has grown up over the years, or sometimes of a sudden influx of anxiety in the family, and it is not hard to see the value of a third party in restoring normal communications.

There are many special circumstances that the parents of a mentally handicapped child must contend with, and it is not surprising if, in a case like Brian's, they are suddenly caught up in a wave of guilt ('How can we tell the school when they have gone to so much trouble over the ATC?'); or even surprise themselves with unexpected feelings ('We were half hoping Brian could stay on at the hostel when we go', or 'I don't know how we are going to face starting all over again in a new town: where will we get help there?'). Sometimes the problem is even more fundamental ('I don't want to go, but my husband will leave me if I don't'). Social work is about nasty surprises like this, mixed feelings, people who don't fit in with society's neater systems; and social workers are there to devise solutions. Sometimes, as with Brian, it is only a matter of releasing a virtual secret and restoring communications. Sometimes it requires something much more complex.

An article in *Social Work Today* (31 March 1981) spoke of a Peter Pan Club — a title that seems to imply no growth, though the club may not. In subtler ways patronising and indeed infantilising practices are still prevalent. There are many reasons for this. First, there is a problem of classification: while they have adult bodies, the mentally handicapped often have children's vocabularies, children's innocence of risks, children's high spirits. This is one of the ways in which they are anomalies — marginal — misfits. It is a common device with all adolescents to press them into one category or another — 'Don't be so childish', 'You are not old enough' — and this process is merely extended with the mentally handicapped. Second, most institutions tend to infantilise their inmates: this is indeed a prime element in the disease of institutional-isation. Long-stay hospitals in particular often develop such practices, in order to control the daily routine of their many patients with the minimum of staff. The best of them mini-mise it, and know of the danger. Special schools, with their wide age range (3–19 in some cases) also risk developing practices which are bad models for teenagers. Again the best of them work very hard to create programmes and involve their older pupils in adult ways. Nor is it unknown for ATCs, with their low staff ratios, to fall into manipulatory ways of 'managing' awkward trainees. These institutional problems have to be tackled sensitively, by carefully reporting impressions after a relationship of trust has been established or, if this has failed, by accepting the need for conflict and working out an effective strategy.

Parents can also be caught up in keeping their child in infancy, as though they needed to keep him in shorts, so to speak. These same parents usually know in their hearts that their child has to grow, and want that to happen – but not yet! There are many understandable reasons, even admirable reasons, for this feeling. If he can stay a child he will not have to face the pain of knowing he is different! Why wake her up when she is happy as she is? We can protect her as long as we are here. But then . . .? 'Then' is the obvious flaw, but there is usually another. Even those who like childhood can see from time to time that there is a different world, and the mentally handicapped are not so blind, nor so daft, that they cannot. Often they sense that they are missing something; that their brothers or sisters get different treatment; that they are encapsulated in someone else's plan for them. In extreme cases, they are actually living a part someone else – usually their parents – has dreamed up for them. They are alienated from themselves and their own wishes, just as some schizophrenics may be. What appears as the odd behaviour of a mentally handicapped person is sometimes the odd behaviour of a schizoid person. In chapter 2 I drew attention to the need of the mentally handicapped to find themselves. But what of the carers? Mannoni (1973) draws attention to the dangers parents – especially mothers – experience when their child begins to improve. This is not just the depression that many mothers experience when the last child starts school, though the sense of loss and uselessness is real. It also contains panic and anxiety about the personal and family problems for which mental handicap has served as scapegoat for some years. Beneath the resistances which parents may put up when change is offered – to a new training programme, short-term care, a camping holiday or placement in a group home, for example – there may lie a longstanding conflict between the parents about caring for the child; and behind that there may lie unresolved anxieties about themselves as individuals. As the child threatens to cut free, the parents are brought back to face these issues which have been dormant for many years. A change for the better also reminds parents of the unceasing pressure of their responsibility. It is relatively easy to live with a vegetable: you know where you are, and can fall into a routine, however wearisome it is. When signs of growth and humanity appear, parents may feel exhausted by the new efforts they must make to encourage them.

There may be other themes, equally complex. If the initial impulse to murder the child was not faced and resolved, it may have recurred time and again in the family's history. Unexplained accidents must be considered in this context, for instance. The mother has often allowed the child to become a parasite on her. For the child to escape into an independent life offers relief, but also the defeat of the mother: the child wins freedom but she does not. On the other hand, parents often project on to a mentally handicapped child parts of themselves that they do not wish to own: he or she comes to symbolise their failures or lacks. If, then, he or she starts to change and refuses to carry these projections, they return to the parents who have to face themselves afresh.

*   *   *

When Gordon left special school he attended the ATC for six months, and was then found a job in a hotel in a neighbouring town, providing accommodation. This was a great success, and for the first time Gordon's parents were on their own. Nothing prevented them restarting the small shop they had always wanted to reopen. They had always blamed Gordon for the failure of the venture six years earlier. Somehow they could not bring themselves to plan for it, however, and were gradually forced to admit that they had not much enjoyed the venture in the first place. They became quite confused about their future and for a time were very depressed.

*   *   *

This is not something that happens to all mentally handicapped people, nor does it have to happen at school-leaving time.

Adolescence brings with it many important changes, any one of which could bring with it a bid for independence. Physical strength may begin to equal that of the parents, sexual feelings may provide a new driving force, mates at work may offer a new model of behaviour, or the ATC programme may put a new emphasis on self-expression. For the child who is seriously repressed and 'spoken for' these are not likely to be strong enough influences for change, but parents can experience anxiety — which may be very great — at this time.

The crucial question in each situation is: what does the change mean in this family? Many difficulties arise because this question is not seriously considered. It should be part of the regular review of each child, but anyway should be started by the time he or she is 15, so that leaving school does not become an urgent crisis. For girls menstruation may precipitate the discussion earlier than this, and it presents the issues in a very clear form. Many parents view the prospect of menstruation as disturbing. They are bothered by the physical hygiene problems and by the difficulty of explaining to their daughter what is happening to her, but much more by having to accept the evidence that she is becoming a physical woman, capable of reproduction. Some feel clear enough in their own minds that this is a function that she will never require, and wish to proceed with sterilisation or a hysterectomy. Others cannot bring themselves to take such a serious decision about another adult life, and some even feel that they must allow for miraculous medical discoveries in the future, which might produce a cure for mental handicap. Society lays down no rules about this, and parents are left to their own resources and to the chance orientation of their advisers of the moment. It is appropriate that the decisions should be taken in the family, and advisers should beware of influencing them strongly one way or the other in accordance with their own prejudices. As with so many similar issues, one of the best ways of exploring the implications is in a group of people who have faced similar dilemmas, and it may be very helpful for parents of mentally handicapped teenagers to have an opportunity of listening to one another's approaches to the problem. They may end up taking quite different decisions, but it will still have been valuable to see the issues from another angle. Social workers can be very helpful in setting up such opportunities.

What happens when we have gone?

Having a mentally handicapped member of their family sometimes makes parents acutely aware of the implications of their own death. This is by no means reserved to older parents, but as they get older they will all be faced more and more squarely with their own non-existence. Many older parents have come through many years during which they had little help to look after their mentally handicapped child, and they have good reason to doubt that society will adequately care for their son or daughter. As their own disabilities increase so does their anxiety about the future. Other members of the family are often hesitant to commit themselves to the kind of burden the parents have borne; but the health and social services are equally reticent if they think that the family might eventually respond. There is therefore a confusing no-man's-land from which it is virtually impossible to see a definite exit route; and this is unsatisfactory from all points of view. It is unsatisfactory for the parents' peace of mind, for the security of the mentally handicapped person, for relationships between the parents and other family members, and not least for social planners. Even if one believes that families should carry 'their own' burdens and should not be too readily relieved of them by the state, there is nothing to be gained by postponing the decision until it is critical. The practical difficulties are that resources have always been so inadequate that it has been impossible to foresee what expedient would have to be adopted at the point of crisis; and that the timing of the crisis itself is so unpredictable.

Ideally, for each mentally handicapped person a structure would be agreed: someone would be recognised as the key decision-maker or trustee, and he or she would remain in close enough contact with the family to be able to reassure them that the future will be secure. This might well be a close member of the family, but where this is not possible for some reason, it could be a social worker, a lawyer, or a trustee appointed by a voluntary organisation. Such a role would have little meaning, however, unless resources are known to be available and the trustee is someone who can influence their allocation. It is because there has been so little prospect of this that parents have attempted to fill the gap. Some local groups have devised their own schemes, or even built hostels. The latter have the problem that they must run full, for economy, and therefore can rarely guarantee a place at a particular time. The NSMHC has also developed a Trusteeship Scheme, into which a mentally handicapped person can be enrolled, and which guarantees a visiting service after the parents' death. Information about this is available through the National Centre, 117–23 Golden Lane, London EC17 0RT. They are also in the process of developing ways of accepting property from parents in exchange for a guarantee of residential provision and care for their mentally handicapped children. Information about the Mencap Homes Foundation, the New Era Housing Association, and Mencap Homeway Ltd can be obtained from the same address.

As with so many of the issues discussed, the exact circumstances will vary from family to family. One couple will worry more about their relatively independent son or daughter than another couple will about their very dependent one. Sometimes brothers or sisters who have been very little involved turn up trumps in a crisis; or others who have promised to help are not available when the time comes. The best reassurance clearly lies in the greatest personal independence, and in lasting relationships with supportive people around each family. Much of the worry that parents feel comes from a realistic doubt that society cares for mentally handicapped people as individuals. It is probably true that virtually none are left with no care when their parents die; and that most adults who require it are received into some form of residential care when their parents become too frail, rather than when they die. However, this happens too often without sensitive planning and personal preparation, so that it is not experienced as individual care; and the parents feel they have failed rather than achieved an important step for their child.

The development of group homes, and of sufficient local

authority hostels to provide a comprehensive network of local residential units (local to each neighbourhood) may eventually create the structure needed to reassure parents. The concept of a 'core and cluster' unit, in which a staffed residential hostel provides the nucleus of a complex of accommodation of many kinds, is now becoming familiar. By its sheer flexibility this pattern of development could go a long way to make it possible to give promises to parents, and to draw mentally handicapped people from the locality into activities at an early stage of their lives, so that when residential care is needed, they can turn to familiar people and to buildings long known to them. Such a structure is likely to work best in urban areas, where staff from the core hostel can keep in easy touch with the surrounding group homes and flats, supported units and independent living accommodation. As Seed (1981) has pointed out in his recent book about the Highlands, things may be less easy in scattered communities. In fact his book scarcely refers to residential accommodation, and it seems that his respondents had a choice only between living at home and going to the central-ised hospital, which might be over 100 miles away. As Peter Mittler says in his introduction to Dr Seed's book:

> Families who are becoming elderly or infirm often struggle hard to keep their adult handicapped son or daughter at home but receive little professional help. Some means has to be found of providing ordinary housing in the community, so that more handicapped adults can leave their parental home when the time comes, rather than have to be admitted to hospital without warning if the family are no longer able to cope . . . even quite seriously handicapped people can continue to live in ordinary houses.

This is certainly true if they are given adequate support by home helps or good neighbours.

4

Relating to Other Relatives

The parents of mentally handicapped children suffer so greatly that it is easy to become preoccupied with their needs and to forget that other members of the family may also be suffering. The fact that many mentally handicapped children are born to older parents means that they will often have older brothers or sisters. Sometimes parents deal with the shock of having had a mentally handicapped child by conceiving again. It is becoming rare in fact to find a single mentally handicapped child. What do other children make of their mentally handicapped brother or sister?

At one level they seem very much less concerned about the handicap itself than adults are. If they are older their first experience is of a baby rather than a damaged person. Much will depend for them on how their parents cope with their own feelings. If they are born later, then their experience is of someone who has always been there, always like that, and reassuringly familiar. There are many accounts of the way in which children accept their handicapped brother or sister, and make them an important part of their lives. Hannam (1975) quotes one who needed his mentally handicapped brother beside him to stop him having bad dreams, and another family where the children were upset when it was suggested that their brother be put into short-term care while the rest of the family had a holiday. Children are often the best interpreters of inarticulateness ('It is very difficult for Mummy and Daddy, because they don't understand him'), and the best comforters of one another. McCormack (1978) gives several examples of families in which the other children have got pleasure from looking after their handicapped brother or sister, from being knowledgeable about their handicap, or from the skill they have developed in picking up non-verbal cues.

This is reassuringly as it should be; but it is not the whole story. First, as Mannoni (1973) indicates, having a mentally handicapped child is like being bereaved. Parents go into mourning, however it is expressed, and everyone in their vicinity is bound to be affected. This may be a temporary phenomenon, but it is quite likely to have a long-term effect on the climate of family life. Second, the sheer slog for parents of bringing up a mentally handicapped child, and the restrictions that this places on the family's social life, are bound to have indirect effects on any other children, older or younger. Third, there are direct effects: duties in relation to the mentally handicapped child, or the impact of his or her behaviour on brothers or sisters; the stigma of being associated with an odd person; inability to do certain things because of his or her needs. Finally, other children have internal reactions to their handicapped brother or sister which can be very powerful: jealousy or protectiveness, aggression or devotion.

The exact form of these pressures depends on the whole shape of the family's life, and the reaction to them will be part of a complex pattern of relationships. We can do no more than draw attention to some possibilities, and witness to the importance of this factor in stressing other children. A newsletter, *Sibs*, has been started to draw attention to their needs, and to offer them a way of coming to terms with their experience.

Parents who are acting as though they are bereaved can have an important impact on their children. Depression is always highly contagious and the children may be affected themselves. But it also means that parents are less available — even if present — for any of their children, that they may not be communicating with one another, and that they may have cut off contact with people outside the family. One may expect all the usual reactions from the children of depressed parents: some — even tiny ones — take over, leading their mother through the daily routine; some take fright and develop night fears, other phobic reactions or enuresis; others again act out, trying to break into the enclosed world of the parents, or to attract attention from outsiders. Depression is not always evident, and when other children in the family of a recently diagnosed mentally handicapped child start to behave in any of these ways, it is worth asking whether the parents have finished their mourning. Some parents who accept the child calmly and seem not to react, are in fact having great difficulty in accommodating what has happened to them, and are inwardly devastated. Such parents may need help to go back and grieve. They can seem frightening people – tense and reserved – to outsiders and may have a similar effect on their children. It requires insight and courage to keep contact with people who are trapped in this way. The tension and fear come from depression which, because it is secret, seems hugely destructive. Despair is never total, however, and the most helpful person is the one who is not afraid of it for him or herself. The person who can accept someone else's depression without being destroyed by it, who can be sad for someone else – cry for them if necessary – and does not have to reassure him or herself that things are all right by cheering everyone up again too quickly, is the one most likely to breach the dikes. Depression is such a common feature of the lives of social work clients that it should be possible to assume that any social worker can handle his/her own reaction to it. This is by no means always the case. Especially in a busy social services department, where the emphasis is on 'service delivery' and getting results, it may be hard for social workers to slow down and feel what is happening to them. When one has a feeling of dread before visiting a family and hopelessness afterwards, it is often a sign that the family is caught up in depression which they cannot handle. The behaviour of the 'other' children in the family can tell the same story.

A more obvious pattern is parental preoccupation with the mentally handicapped member. His or her needs may be very demanding and their emotional response to the child may, in addition, be highly protective. They may be having to learn how to respond effectively to a child who gives unusual cues. They may have unconsciously reinforced demanding behaviour which keeps them at full stretch. In situations like this, other children are also likely to become more demanding, if they have hope for themselves; or may find patterns of behaviour – for example, losing toilet training, making other messes, or stealing – which compete with those of the handicapped child. If children lose hope for themselves, they may become depressed or ill, or look for support outside the family. In large families they can sometimes find substitute parents, in grandparents or even in children near their own age; but in a small family with perhaps only two children, the plight of the second may be quite acute. At one extreme, the non-handicapped child may be entirely rejected and placed for adoption or in care.

In one family, a baby of 2 years appeared to stop developing as soon as he reached the attainments of his 7-year-old brother who was mentally handicapped. In another, a 1-year-old girl became very difficult to handle because she was so excited by the antics of her mentally handicapped brother. In both cases the parents were by no means indifferent to the needs of the second child; were in fact very dejected by their failure to protect them, but felt they must give priority to the child in deepest need and could not provide the special attention that the second required.

Jealousy of the handicapped child may sometimes take a direct form and produce hostile behaviour; or it may be converted into over-solicitousness or emulation. As always, the response of parents to behaviour of this kind will be crucial. If they react in ways which encourage it – even by punishment – it may become part of a pattern which is hard to eradicate. In some cases, where the parents have become locked up in their own feelings, in particular have not managed to resolve their anger and depression and cannot talk about it, another child may become the vehicle for expressing the parents' feelings, or may be the principal victim. This may take the form of acting out – drawing the attention of people outside the family to the stresses that exist, by pestering neighbours, disrupting school activities or by outright crime. It may equally take the form of individual suffering – loss of performance at school, sickness or merely failure to thrive. It is important for teachers, doctors, social workers and others to be on the alert for problems of this kind in children from families with a handicapped member.

The direct effects of having a handicapped brother or sister can also be very extreme. In one family with a hyperactive boy, it proved necessary to keep every door in the house locked so that he could not vent his energies uncontrolled. Living in such a strange environment made it very hard for his brother and sister to bring friends home — a common deprivation. Having to spend time supervising the handicapped child is another common penalty for ordinary children. Many have suffered physically, especially if they are younger children — some being regularly attacked for no obvious reason. Some families have been unable to have holidays. Others have had to move house, disrupting the ordinary children's schooling, so as to be near a good special school. Most children feel some sense of stigma because of their damaged sibling and have been teased at school. And this is often internalised as a worry about one's own mental state: 'Perhaps there is something wrong with me too.' This can affect the confidence with which brothers and sisters cope with school difficulties of a quite ordinary kind, and later it can affect the way they present themselves when looking for a marriage partner. They know that other people are anxious about genetic defects and cannot free themselves of the slur. When they do get married, they have to make decisions about how far they will be involved, and will involve their families, with their handicapped brother or sister. And finally there is the extension of that problem: what happens when their parents have gone or can no longer cope? This issue can cause tension between the parents and all their children, between the children themselves, and between the children and their spouses. Guilt about not doing one's duty can weigh heavily for the whole of one's adult life if the family pressures are directed that way. These difficulties are all rooted in reality. There are others which are less rational.

Children sometimes blame themselves for the damage their brother or sister shows, however irrational this may seem. Rivalry is normal in any family, but if one's rival is damaged it is sometimes hard to avoid feeling guilty. Anyone who has worked with children who have damaged or sick parents will know how important it is to take such feelings seriously. Unresolved, they can be the basis of much anxiety and depression later on. Often this is only apparent in over-concern for the handicapped person. The brother or sister devotes him- or herself to helping and caring, and may gain a great deal of satisfaction and reward from this. Part of this concern may again come from guilt: 'Why should I be all right when he is like that?' or 'How can I complain about my life when I look at her?' Sometimes the ordinary children are caught up in irrational feelings that come from their parents. Some feel that they have been expected to be perfect to make up for the loss in the damaged brother or sister. Some have been spoiled by parents who felt guilty about the deprivations they have had to impose on their other children. Some have lived in a slightly mad world where the handicap was denied by one or both parents – 'We were not supposed to notice.'

The list could go on indefinitely. Each family is a constellation of individuals and they work differently on one another. What is clear is that while some families may be drawn together by having a mentally handicapped child, if there is any existing tension or an unfortunate coincidence of problems or stress on an individual, then the additional burden of having a mentally handicapped child can induce great risks for one or another member. Mostly the focus is on the parents, but in some families, and in all families sometimes, it may fall on one of the other children. Two examples sum this up well.

*   *   *

Jonathan was born three years after his mentally handicapped brother. He did not thrive, was often upset by his brother's behaviour and was late to develop speech (like his brother). He looked an anxious, pale child and did badly at school. When he was 9, his brother was transferred to a residential school and Jonathan immediately blossomed. In six months he had lost his peaky, worried expression and was a normal relaxed child. At school he began to catch up and has emerged as a good average pupil. He seldom mentions his brother.

*   *   *

Mary was the eldest of four children, of whom the third was a mentally handicapped boy. At the age of 15 she began to stay away from home more and more. When her parents remonstrated she accused them of spoiling her life because she could never have friends. They were caught on the raw by this and found it hard to exercise any further control.

Mary stayed away, sometimes for days on end, often did not go to school and made no attempt to reassure her parents as to where she had been. Eventually she was arrested for shop-lifting and asked the probation officer to arrange for her to go into care. She could not bear to be at home because she felt so bad about her parents' life, but was not able yet to cope on her own. Foster parents were found and Mary stayed uneventfully with them for two years.

*   *   *

What can a social worker do to help? The specific ways depend on the family, but there are a number of general points to be made. First, they can keep the interests of the other children alive through the critical early period, when so much attention has to be paid to the handicapped baby and its meaning for the parents. If there are older children, parents may be slow to see that they are being neglected, relatively speaking. By asking about their way of coping and providing information about common reactions in other children, the social worker may be able to draw the parents' attention to the needs of the others too.

Second, the social worker can sometimes offer a direct opportunity for the other children to talk about their feelings. This can be done quite informally, in asides almost, or through play material, while talking with the parents. Occasionally it may be valuable to take the children out or arrange for them to come for a talk on their own. More often than is usual, it would be helpful to draw them into a family discussion where their specially acute view of events can often cut through adult nonsense.

*   *   *

I don't know why Mummy gets so upset about Robin shouting. It keeps him happy and I know Mrs Boreham next door doesn't mind, 'cause you can hardly hear it in there. But she gets all worked up, and then takes it out on all of us, and Dad. I think he ought to stop her more.

*   *   *

A useful book by Sobol (1978), written as by a young girl, explores quite gently many of the feelings mentioned above.

Another, valuable for explaining mental handicap to quite small children is Larsen (1974).

Third, it is important to try and ensure that the family maintains its outside links. This may involve only practical help with transport and baby-sitting, but it can also mean putting pressure on the parents to stay socially involved. The temptation to reduce outside contacts is often very great. As depression sets in, confidence wanes and exhaustion builds up. Other people provide moments of hope and a different standard from the parental one, and are very necessary for children who are under stress. For the same reasons it is equally important to ensure that the family gets holidays, or at least that the other children get away. Some families will prefer to put the mentally handicapped child into short-term care and go away together; others to send the other children away on their own. Either may meet with resistance from the other children: 'He is our brother and we want him with us.' It may, however, be important for them to get an experience of life without handicap so that their daily life falls into perspective.

We are not talking only about brothers and sisters who are children. Reference has already been made to the way that adult brothers and sisters may be affected – in their self-image, in their marriage partners and in their marriages. Bayley found that a significant number of the mentally handicapped who were unmarried, whose parents had died, and who had brothers and sisters, were in fact living with them (or had done so before going into institutional care). In the case of the mildly handicapped the figure was 38 per cent, but for the severely handicapped it was as high as 51 per cent and 85 per cent for those living outside institutions (Bayley, 1973, app. A, table A4). When one recognises that some will have moved away from the area by the time of their parents' death and some will have died themselves, it is clear that siblings provide an important care resource for mentally handicapped people. Their own families may in turn be burdened, and their children affected by having a mentally handicapped aunt or (less often) uncle living with them; although in the majority of cases the children will be growing up before the burden falls upon the family. Such families need the same range of supports that the original families needed and should be linked up in the same way with supportive organisations.

Children are not the only relatives who are closely affected by the birth of a handicapped baby. Grandparents may also be touched very personally. For them the impact may not be so great but many will experience the loss of their future quite keenly, especially if the first grandchild is involved. They can be in a key position to help, or to make matters worse; much depends on the relationship they already have with their own children and in-laws. They usually hold a crucial symbolic position, as the first people to be told about the baby. When the diagnosis has been made at once, the parents may still be in a state of shock themselves when they break the news and may hear, in the grandparents' reaction, a verdict from society on their 'failure'. In extreme cases grandparents have been shocked into saying crass things: 'Well, it didn't come from our side of the family'; 'I said you shouldn't have married her'; 'You should never have had another one.'

Grandparents need to find their own explanation for a misfortune that has come too close to them. They are threatened by the fact that there is a genetic link; and it is usually possible on every family tree, of which they are the custodians, to find a branch on which the problem can be hung. Guilt is not then far away, and whether they accept it or reject it they can find themselves in considerable pain. Some will blame themselves: 'We should have known, because of Madge's boy.' Some will blame their son or daughter: 'You must be being punished for something.' Some will push the blame on to the other side of the family: 'She ought never to have been smoking when she was carrying'; 'Well, we know our Bob is all right . . . .' Some will vent it on the health services: 'They shouldn't have given her all those pills.'

Whatever explanation they choose, it is likely to be dissonant with the one the parents have chosen. Younger generations not only have different conceptual systems, they also have a need to distance themselves from their parents. The time of one's own parenthood is a critical moment for this, especially with one's first child. One is proving one's own worth, taking up the baton, sustaining the family's pride and 'undefiled heritage' doing as well as one's parents — the symbolism is very tangled. A damaged child then carries a meaning through the generations and affects relationships of every kind. When relationships have been good anyway, they can be strengthened by such a trial; but where there is already some tension, it is likely to be inflamed.

Some parents cannot admit that their child is handicapped and obscure the fact from grandparents as long as possible. Others who are not admitting it, even to themselves, may create a gross problem for their parents, who sense what is coming but dare not speak about it. Sometimes grandparents are themselves so affected by the news that they cannot share their feelings and cut themselves off. Parents may then have to cope with the burden of having hurt their parents as well as with their own pain, which may distress or anger them, according to their usual relationship. And there may be complicating circumstances, like grandparents who are ill already, or recently bereaved, or depressed by their own decline. But grandparents can also be enormously reassuring, conveying that the world will go on and that other people have lived through worse things. As with all children, grandparents can take enjoyment where parents get annoyance, and in doing so can show parents that it is possible. They can provide an acceptable place to leave the handicapped child when it seems that no one else could understand, and a safe refuge from the handicapped child for battered parents or the other children. As time goes on they can provide a witness for growth and development, seeing the child at intervals and noticing the imperceptible changes that parents cannot see. It is worth a great deal to maintain this relationship and social workers will sometimes be in a position to help this to happen. In particular, it will be worth checking how grandparents have taken the news in the early stages and, if they are accessible, making an offer of counselling to them. They need information almost as much as the parents do and are often in a much worse position to get it, living with dated fears. Much of their information must come through the parents, but it may be difficult for them to pose some of their questions without stirring up doubts and resentments in the parents: 'George used to run around with a bad girl. Could he have caught something?' 'His wife's aunt was in the asylum for three years. Don't you think there's a tendency on their side?' 'What is it going to do to them? Wouldn't they be better putting the child away?'

It requires sensitivity to know when such a direct contact with the older generation will be acceptable to the parents, and when it will cause suspicion and anxiety. It should not, in ordinary circumstances, be undertaken without their knowledge. Sometimes it will be more appropriate and rewarding to suggest having a discussion with the whole family, and to bring into the open the fears and feelings that have been suppressed. Any family crisis tends to reveal the stress lines in relationships, and offers a chance to understand them and rearrange them more constructively. It is not always possible to use a crisis in this way, because defences are too high or because key people are not available to join the family review. But the opportunity should always be considered so as to maintain the resource that grandparents represent.

As time goes on and grandparents become frail or handicapped in their own right, they may become a second burden for the parents. It is not uncommon now for parents in their 60s to have the worry of a son or daughter around 40, and of their own parents in their 80s. The combination can be very crippling, especially if all three generations have to live together. The elderly can feel that they are deprived of their due care and attention because of the mentally handicapped person, while the latter may resent the presence of his or her grandparents; and the parents are torn between the two.

This is not a problem specific to mental handicap and it should not be assumed that mentally handicapped people cannot help to support older people in need. Where this constellation of generations appear, social workers should be alert for ways of helping the grandparents, as a way of reducing stress all round. When the grandparents are at a distance, their influence may be hidden, but they may be causing a great deal of anxiety for the parents. It may be necessary to indicate to the latter that even specialist social workers are interested in all the problems that impinge on them, and to ensure that their problems are not dealt with in isolation from one another.

The whole of this chapter is an argument for a family approach to social work with mentally handicapped people. Although people are sometimes split off from their families by divorce, rehousing or institutionalisation; although some people live in units that are not the conventional nuclear family; and although families often feel closer to friends than to kin – the blood tie has a way of reasserting itself at times of stress and most people use their 'familiar' family members as reference points, ways of checking their own identity and of hearing what the world thinks. For many they are also a reliable source of help – not without emotional strings, of course – and of support which is blind to at least some of one's faults. For these reasons alone it is worth trying to keep family relationships in working order and to make them as productive as possible. Mental handicap affects all family members; the mentally handicapped member is in turn affected by all the other things that are going on in his or her family; the other family members affect each other; and everyone has concerns which affect no one else in the family. The social worker who is doing a fully competent job will be sensitive to the interweaving of all these strands, but will not make the mistake of assuming that they all originate in the mentally handicapped person. This is the characteristic mistake of people who work with only one family member or with one kind of problem. It is a danger with all specialists, because they start from a particular vantage point and are good at seeing things clearly from that vantage point. Social workers are accustomed to working with family members other than the 'focal' one: they often have responsibility for reminding residential staff or specialist consultants that other members of the family have reasons for what they do, and are not just intrusions on the smooth pattern of 'therapeutic' events. They often have to assert that a world exists outside the hospital, residential home, clinic or school, which has its own pressures and logic; and that the individual patient, resident or pupil is just one actor in that world. A family crisis is always a group process, involving many people and their hopes and fears. They all have to be seen as participants, and the crisis can never be resolved — although sometimes an emergency can be defused — by dealing only with one person. Social work concerns not just the mentally handicapped person and his or her parents, but siblings, grandparents, aunts, uncles, cousins, in-laws and courtesy family members. It also concerns whatever constellation of professional people has formed around the family.

5

Relating to Other Professionals

It is evident from much that has been said in earlier chapters that social work with mentally handicapped people is not an isolated enterprise. This follows from the fact that the primary services required by mentally handicapped people and their families are provided by the health service and the education service; and from the key role that the ATC plays for so many adults. It follows naturally enough from the fact that social work is about anomalies in other systems, and from the whole normalisation argument, which proposes that mentally handicapped people should be helped through the ordinary agencies of social life which are available to the public at large.

Social workers usually belong to a team of some kind: it may be a multi-disciplinary team in a hospital, or a team of only social workers in a geographical area. Even those who do not have immediate colleagues in their own employment setting usually find themselves working in close alliance with a few other professionals whose area of concern, geographical or specialist or both, overlaps their own. Teamwork in this narrow sense is therefore built into the job, and the problems of working effectively in one's own immediate team are very significant to good practice.

Because each individual client and each family will require a different combination of services, social workers find themselves working with varied groupings of people at different times in the working week. A hospital social worker may, for instance, be working at one moment with a doctor and a psychologist in an assessment clinic for children whose development appears retarded; the same afternoon she may be talking with a teacher in the hospital school and nurses from a children's ward. The next day she may be discussing a short-term placement with a social worker and teacher from outside the hospital. Similarly, a group home organiser might be engaged one day in a training programme at the ATC with a nurse from a hospital which had placed patients in the pro-gramme. The next day he might be involved at a group home with a housing welfare officer and the local clergyman trying to work out how best to involve neighbours in helping with practical problems about the house. It is an overstatement to call all these transient working relationships 'teamwork', but often they contain the seeds of longer-term collaboration, if the various workers can allow their common interests to predominate over their mutual suspicions, and can share their anxieties instead of merely defending themselves. This is a delicate chemistry, and a social worker is not an effective professional until he or she has learned the necessary skills to help it to happen.

Not the least of these collaborative relationships is the one that involves the mentally handicapped person and his or her family and friends. They are the team who are closest to the ground and who have to make work whatever suggestions and resources are offered by other people. In a sense the other teams draw their meaning and indeed their existence from the relationships around their individual mentally handicapped clients, and nothing that goes on in the other teams is wholly irrelevant to them. If the others are depressed, having affairs with one another, or projecting memories of their parents on to one another, this is likely to have some backwash on their mentally handicapped clients, and it can sometimes produce a tidal wave of bad feelings and public recrimination.

This is always clearest in residential settings, where relation-ships are more concentrated and there is more opportunity to observe encounters face to face. This does not mean that similar relationships and their consequences do not occur elsewhere. The discussion of such problems in the therapeutic community movement in hospitals (M. Jones, 1968 and 1976), in the planned environment movement in residential schools (Wills, 1971), in the thinking of residential social workers, and in the analysis of institutions (Miller and Gwynne, 1972) has been rich if not voluminous. Balint's work (1964) did a similar job for doctors working in the open community. In general, however, people are very slow to use these insights, for the simple reason that they demand in Maxwell Jones's term, 'painful communication'. Any rich relationship involves pain, or the risk of pain. Working with people who are already in pain, physically or emotionally, threatens to double the dose. Work with mentally handicapped people is therefore fraught with two kinds of burden: the burden one is sharing with mentally handicapped people themselves, and the helpers' reactions, which include too much of themselves to hide but too much to reveal. However sophisticated one tries to be, one is often put on the spot of one's own weaknesses because of the basic nature of the problem, whether it is daily survival, sexual experiment or human rejection, and by the removal of so many of the devices by which we normally communicate or disguise our true feelings.

Menzies (1960) drew attention to such problems, but they have still not been sufficiently recognised. The business of helping the handicapped is full of pain which we ignore at our peril. Some of the sources of this pain have been reviewed in earlier chapters. We are interested here in the effect it has on working relationships between colleagues; and in the complex ways in which it is transformed into individual defences and organisational structure. A great deal of what passes for efficient systems is really little more than a defence against pain, chaos and despair. We are each rather blind to this in our own service, and believe that we have organised ourselves rationally to help our clients; but in other people's structures we can often see very clearly the dysfunctional elements — the defences against 'our' clients. Then we feel provoked and morally indignant, and professional relationships are soured. In this way each professional, and each professional service, can be a threat to every other: we threaten to expose one another's defences and put heavier demands on one another than each of us can contain. This is a central factor in referrals, in case conferences and in the handling of crises. In each of these situations we have both the client and the realities of service resources in mind; but we are also reacting to our personal pain thresholds and sometimes — consciously or unconsciously — to the pain thresholds of people for whom we feel responsible, like junior colleagues.

A referral from one service to another may be a wholly rational act, but this is rare. Just occasionally two services have agreed their respective functions and a client who cannot, or can no longer be helped by one is transferred to the other with general satisfaction. More often functions are rather ill-defined: they overlap somewhat or there is a gap which no one fills, and therefore there is room for dispute about where the client 'belongs'. Alternatively, one or other service feels aggrieved at the definition of its role and resists work which is within its prescribed function. Or again, it has come under a great deal of temporary pressure and can no longer cope with its agreed share of the work. A referral, then, is often a political act — an attempt to renegotiate the relationship between two services — as well as a therapeutic one. Often this political dimension is not wholly conscious: the two services are operating with different ideas of how they should work together and each referral merely reflects the perceptions of the referrer; but is experienced by the recipient as a threat — as pressure to change. This is particularly true at a time when values are being reconsidered and the roles of organisations are shifting. Before a new consensus has been achieved, some people will start to act on their own ideas of what it should be. This is inevitable and sometimes happens unconsciously, but may at times be accompanied by reforming zeal which makes it all the harder for the respondent to react positively.

Often a referral expresses the personal pain and discomfort of the referrer. However justifiable, failure is implied — an inability to help, except by invoking another agent — and it may be necessary to the referrer's peace of mind that the case be accepted. This may be on the level of personal limitation ('I don't know enough about brain damage') or lack of resources ('I don't have time to give him what he needs'), but it may also be on the level of interpersonal conflict ('We have reached the end of our tether with her: the staff will all leave if she does not') or organisational failure ('We aren't doing him any good: we just don't have the trained staff or continuity'). Again, the referral may be inspired by pressure from someone else: parents who are unhappy with the treatment or education their child is getting; neighbours who have alarmed a GP about the lifestyle of someone living independently; or councillors who have had a complaint. A referral is some sort of cry for help, but it is often hard to be clear what its implications are and they need careful unravelling. Every referral indicates the existence of a crisis — someone wants something changed — but the form in which the referral is presented does not always indicate where the crisis lies. Often the tension that is created when a referral is turned down comes from failure to identify the real crisis, and from treating the communication at face value.

*   *   *

Life in a residential hostel became rather difficult when a young outsider was appointed officer in charge over the head of the older existing deputy. The new head of the hostel introduced more relaxed ideas about its running, and encouraged the male and female residents to mix more freely. The deputy was rather shocked by this and tried to hold on to the previous rules when she was on duty. She made much of any problems which the new regime produced and voiced her criticism to parents when they visited. One girl of 18 was found one night in the room of a 26-year-old man, and when confronted by the deputy the next day, attacked her physically. The deputy insisted that she should be transferred to the local mental handicap hospital on the grounds that she was too difficult to be contained in the hostel; and the head felt too insecure to prevent it. The hospital turned the referral down. Three days later, when the head and deputy were both on duty, the girl made a great show of kissing and cuddling with her boyfriend. The deputy protested, and when the head refused to do anything she walked out and wrote a letter to the Director of Social Services, complaining that the girl was inappropriately placed and that the hospital had been unhelpful. The Director took the matter up with the hospital consultant, who rejected his approach fairly brusquely. Some days later the girl cut her hand in circumstances which suggested that she had done it deliberately. Eventually the consultant offered to come down to the hostel. The girl described her uncertainty about what was permitted with the new regime at the hostel, and in a long session the head and deputy talked about their mistrust of one another, and their difficulty in resolving how political issues should be handled when they felt so out of touch philosophically. It was agreed that the social worker from the hospital would attend the weekly staff meetings for a few months to help to keep the discussions open; and things slowly settled down again.

*   *   *

In this case the referrals to the hospital appear to have been quite inappropriate, unless one interprets them as an appeal to a helpful group of people for intervention, not in the girl's life but in that of the hostel staff. The attitude of the Director of Social Services appears to confirm their need to go outside the usual management structure; and the final response of the hospital managed to put the emphasis where it belonged. One can see, however, that the hospital staff might easily have responded literally a third time and become embroiled in a testy discussion about how to handle difficult teenagers or scarce resources. There is often no time for more than a literal response ('Her behaviour does not justify our trans- ferring her here'); and if people in different services are not accustomed to sharing the anxiety of their work, it may not even seem appropriate to look below the surface. The stan- dard bureaucratic attitude would be: 'I have no business to interfere in the local authority's management problems (or the hospital's internal problems).' This kind of compart- mentalising is very bad for morale because it creates an atmosphere of rejection and secrecy, and limits the resources available for problem-solving.

Very similar issues arise in many case conferences, when people come clinging to their departmental loyalties instead of opening their minds to the client's needs and their mutual dependence. A case conference is called to resolve problems which are about agency functions as well as individual clients. There is nothing wrong with that: different agencies are established to look at problems from different angles, and this means that they cannot always reconcile their views easily. The rational basis for a case conference is this reconciliation of differing professional viewpoints. However, many other factors also become involved. A case conference is usually initiated because one person or one agency is unhappy about what they believe is happening. In this sense there is a crisis at the heart of a case conference also. Once one starts asking,

'Why are we here?', 'Who wants what changed?', 'What is going on between us?', as well as 'What is the matter with this man?' or 'What are we going to do with him?', the discussion can move into channels which are much more productive. It ought to be possible to assume that people in different services will have different values and perceptions of a set of events by virtue of their professional roles, and that a meeting like a case conference will be needed from time to time to review these differences and try to find a way of resolving them by adjusting the roles. Unfortunately the discussion is so often approached and experienced, by one party or another, as a personal threat, that it gets bogged down. Here again, as with referrals, there is a paradox: so long as the discussion focuses only on its 'proper' task, it often seems to get blocked with these irrational elements. Yet if the irrational elements can be admitted to the discussion, it then often becomes possible to resolve the task issues. Organisations, therefore, which only deal with the official agenda, tend to produce a good deal of frustration and tension in their members, even if formal decisions get made; and are often subject to unexpected eruptions of feeling or misbehaviour because there is no official way of recognising emotional issues — the hidden agenda.

Most social workers will understand what I am talking about, because they have had some exposure to irrational behaviour and know it must be taken seriously, if not always at face value. They are likely, in their work with clients, to give due place to hidden agendas: to wait for people to bring out the comment they have been suppressing, to help to put the unspoken into words, and to place secrets on the table. But they are much less ready to do the same in their relationships with colleagues. No doubt this is due in part to a tendency for social workers to be people who prefer to manage others than to be managed themselves. It is reinforced by the isolation of the social worker in action: like teachers, they operate in a social situation but no one except their clients knows what each of them actually does. A factor which may now be stronger than either of these is their employment, for the most part, in large bureaucratic organisations which place little importance on feelings and personal relationships, and attempt to rely on written definitions (job descriptions, policy guidelines, rulebooks, operational briefs) to control their work. It is important to state as clearly as possible what an organisation is trying to do and on what criteria it will be making its decisions. But the only organisations which can rely on these alone are those which operate in a static environment — make a definite product in a specific way, using fixed materials and unchanging labour, for a known group of consumers. Anything less like social work it would be hard to imagine! The social worker's job is to identify people whose needs are not being met by regular social processes; to invent new ways of meeting their needs, using whatever resources or devices come to hand; to do this in a climate of changing social values; and at times to try to change that climate. Fixed procedures will not therefore be enough. It is essential to create an environment in which people can share ill-formed ideas, introduce feelings into formal agendas, consider how personalities are affecting role and task performance, and discuss professional relationships as a necessary part of the work. Without this it will be very hard to break out of the procedural strait-jacket which gives security at the price of stifling creativity and producing frustration. This applies to communication within a single unit — a ward, hostel, ATC or school; it applies to relationships between units — an ATC and its feeder schools, a hostel and the hospital that backs it; and it applies to communications within whatever planning forums exist in each locality. It has to be possible to ask, 'Why are your people so tetchy at the moment?' and to say, 'Things are not very good with us just now: don't ask us to help for a bit.'

This is the reality which lies beneath the concept of the Community Mental Handicap Team, proposed by the National Development Group (1977a). It is a cool proposal which conceals a turbulent reality. It is not any the less valid for that, but we must beware of allowing it to become one of those administrative ghosts which seems to exist because it has been suggested — 'We are doing that anyway.' The hard fact is that teamwork only happens in any setting when the team members can look at one another squarely and share their doubts, not only about each other which is hard enough, but about themselves.

I hope I have not given the impression that good teamwork is a matter of good personal relationships alone. This is not the whole story. There have been many people who got on well enough on the golf course or in the social club, but could not develop their work. In a sense I want to give the opposite impression. In the real world people do not become good friends very easily, and it is a more common experience that one's colleagues are awkward and self-willed, or passive and ineffectual, thoughtless, interfering or neurotic. And from their point of view one is no different. This is the raw material of teamwork! If friendship were a prerequisite of teamwork there would be very little teamwork. So collaboration starts between ill-assorted partners. In an army it may be possible to drill each individual so that he fits in to a pre-designed role and plays a part according to other people's expectations. In many institutional settings, however, these roles cannot be predesigned and team members must initially negotiate their individual roles, which then become established and understood — 'understood', that is, as someone else's territory, as routine ways of performing particular tasks and as ends in themselves. Some valuable human insights may then get lost.

It takes a sharp-eyed occupational therapist to see, when she comes on to a ward, that a cleaner who is allowing a patient to interfere with her work may be doing a better job of training in daily living than the OT programme which is on the notice board. It needs a sister with unusual self-awareness to see that the male patient who hangs around the female ward is actually helping to get her patients up in the morning, and is daily improving his own appearance into the bargain. Someone not connected with the ward and its routines may spot the results at once. Similarly, the minibus driver who provides the physical link between home and school may be an important commentator at either end on why a particular pupil seems so miserable, or why a particular teacher is so unpopular. The ATC instructor could often explain why a particular social worker's visits are fruitless. And the GP often has a shrewd idea why a consultant can feel fond, and can therefore help one patient and not another. These observations, which go on below the level of the formal 'task', are not for that reason written into job descriptions, and often deliberately excluded from professional recognition, and yet abound in every relationship, in every setting. There is more to be learned from what ward orderlies say over their coffee or a school caretaker says in the cloakrooms, than from many diagnostic assessments and case conferences. They observe, uninhibitedly, the actual interactions of the supposed high and the supposed low, and can say what they see. But unless their comments are shared, they are of no use.

The same applies exactly to supposed sophisticated conversations. Teachers and psychologists, social workers and nurses, doctors and housing staff, can all see what is going on with one another – at least from their own point of view. Two of them know that a third has trouble with the Smith family, because he cannot cope with aggression. He knows that the school is being taken for a ride, because the staff are too inclined to take offence and will not listen to parents' suggestions. The school sees that the ATC manager is trying to have a quiet life for his last few years. And the ATC laughs because the hospital nurses have no idea how to train their patients for everyday life. And no one says any of these things except covertly. These sharp insights on individuals are effectively lost and the system grinds collusively on. People protect one another against painful communication, so as to ward off similar communications that might be addressed to themselves and cling to their convenient half-truths.

The mistake usually made at this point of the discussion is to imply that defence mechanisms are wrong and that anxiety, anger and despair are signs of weakness and inefficiency. Perhaps they would be in an ideal world, but in this imperfect one we must assume that people have weaknesses and therefore need defences. The last thing we want is to drive the weaknesses underground so that they cannot be discussed openly, or to make the defences secret. Let us accept that if our colleagues are dealing with the pain and despair of their clients, patients, pupils or trainees, then they will at times become ragged and unresponsive, nervy and aggressive – and will see the same happening to us. There are two possible ways on from that point: one is to put up defensive barriers so that one is not contaminated by other people's stress; the other is to treat the stress as a mutual problem and try to reduce it by joint action. There can be no doubt that the latter approach is more rational; but this does not make it any easier to achieve, and it is more common to find people who are in the same boat fighting one another rather than looking for the common enemy. This phenomenon occurs at every level and is the antithesis of teamwork: it can undermine not only collaboration between services but morale in each service. It is a considerable contribution to the services as a whole when anyone calls a halt to the construction of Maginot lines and seeks to create a common front.

Examples of this fundamental human problem could be drawn from the behaviour of people in lifeboats, or at disarmament conferences. In the field of mental handicap the same issues emerge in the relationship of two care assistants in a hostel, two wards in a hospital, a special school and an ATC, between a mental handicap hospital and the SSD, between two county councils, or between statutory and voluntary bodies. All these individuals and agencies operate within a common field – that of service to mentally handicapped people. Each has limited resources; the field as a whole is deprived and the most common battles occur on internal boundaries. There is a place for conflict, obviously. All people need defence systems, and it would be idealistic folly to think that they could be removed overnight or completely. Therefore there will sometimes be a need for a frontal assault or for undermining the walls. Far more often, however, the walls would simply fall into ruins if a real attempt was made to understand the reasons for different philosophies and for an inequitable distribution of resources.

Here are some examples of 'Maginot' thinking that have come my way:

*   *   *

The night care assistant in a hostel complained that she was always left with too much work to do because the day staff did not get residents off to bed soon enough. She insisted that they should all be in their rooms by ten o'clock, so that she could get on with checking security and the rest of her tasks. The day staff protested that this would interfere with the hostel's policy of giving residents more say in their own lives, and refused to co-operate. The night care assistant made her protest by refusing to get residents up in time to dress before the day staff came on duty. This continued for three days before a staff meeting could be called, and led to increasingly tense exchanges between the two groups. The night staff became more and more unpopular with residents also, who found ways of making the evenings very difficult — staying out late, quarrelling about the television and demanding food. One or two had fits, and the night care assistant scalded herself one evening while making tea. Eventually the issues were discussed at the staff meeting. The problem was the familiar one of policy changes being made during the day-time without proper discussion with the night staff, who were therefore thrust into an obstructive role when they raised objections. The importance of bed-time was recognised by everyone, whereas only the night staff had seen this before, and an overlap of day staff was arranged to make it possible to help residents sensitively with their preparations for bed. The recriminations ceased at once and a good deal of acting out at bed-time, which had been accepted as normal, also died away.

*   *   *

A mental handicap hospital unilaterally announced that it would take no more admissions for holiday relief. This caused a storm of protest from local authority and voluntary organisations, and great anxiety to individual parents. The hospital insisted that it could not provide adequate staff for its basic functions and must therefore curtail additional activities. The nursing budget was in fact insufficient to cover the number of posts allocated to the hospital. The public criticism which followed made the staff bitter and depressed for a time. Only gradually was there acceptance that they had a case and that they needed support in their fight for more resources.

*   *   *

A county council which had planned a residential hostel for mentally handicapped people for many years, kept having to put it back in the building programme. The local voluntary society grew increasingly exasperated. When the county council found itself with a house on its hands and proposed to make it into a group home, the society was therefore highly suspicious. They reacted with hostility and cast doubt on the whole idea of group homes. Battle was joined on the question of whether suitable candidates existed for an unstaffed home, and whether external support would be adequate.

*   *   *

In all three of these cases the various parties had a clear common interest to obtain resources or provide services for mentally handicapped people; yet conflict broke out which damaged, at least temporarily, the common goal. It is important to recognise that in each case one party at least was under special pressure and felt its interests were not appreciated by other people. It does not matter whether other people did understand their position: this had not been communicated, so the tension remained. It is also important to recognise that the other parties involved felt they were behaving reasonably: the day staff thought they were developing a new approach to self-care; the district management team thought it was managing its nursing budget to the best interests of all; and the county council thought it was adding a new resource. Yet conflict emerged. It is not enough to say that communications were not good enough. That is trite and true, but one has to ask why they were not good enough. What was it, in each case, that prevented concerned people from sharing their hopes and frustrations?

It was not simply a question of philosophy. It is very easy when conflicts arise between services which have different orientations to believe that the argument is ideological – the medical model versus the educational one! Crisis intervention versus behaviour modification! It is rarely so simple, and attempts to resolve the problem on ideological grounds alone rarely succeed. People adopt the ideology and philosophy which suit them; they become closely identified with them for that reason and are not likely to give them up lightly. This does not mean that there is no room for co-operation. Most problems occur because people are dismissive, consciously or unconsciously, of one another's beliefs; and because they are less than wholly willing to explain their own beliefs, and discover what is fundamental and what is non-essential in them. On the contrary, people with very different ideologies can often work together well if they are talking to one another as people, and recognise one another's humanity. This can overcome the handicap that their ideologies present to each of them and to one another. Indeed, every lesson that one learns about communication with mentally handicapped people is relevant to relationships with one's colleagues! They are whole human beings, who have feelings as well as tasks to perform. By listening carefully to their confused utterances and watching for small signals of pleasure and understanding, one can begin to grasp the meaning of events for them. This is often different from the meaning one creates for oneself, and even from the conventional meaning; and it can explain their otherwise strange behaviour.

I am not really joking. It pays enormous dividends to try to understand why professional colleagues behave in the way they do. Sometimes this can help one to see events in a fresh and helpful light; sometimes it is useful to colleagues if they are asked to express their views as clearly as they can, and to discover where theory and practice separate; sometimes it simply creates an atmosphere in which frustrations can be shared and self-doubt admitted.

There are many ways of working towards this end and they are all familiar to caseworkers. The first is openness and honesty in communication. If one service is failing or in difficulties, it is important to admit this frankly so that others know where they are, can make accommodation for the failure and may even help. 'Keeping up the image' by public relations methods is in the long run self-defeating because it alienates support and undermines corporate action. If this sounds heretical, it merely demonstrates how far we have strayed from openness and honesty in the recent years of large organisations. The second way is face-to-face contact. The more people from one service work together with those of another, the quicker the ideologies fall away and people are seen as human beings. When tension starts to appear in a relationship, it is high time to ask the service in question to ask one over for a day, or to collaborate in some common venture. Work is better than observation, but any common enterprise can relax and humanise a relationship. Time spent helping to organise a jumble sale or planning an outing can do more for the next referral than pages of memoranda. The third way is regularity of contact. It is hard to do the difficult things in a relationship — admitting one's failures, asking about someone else's, raising an objection or sharing a suspicion — unless there is a chance for reparation at a later date. If people know they will meet again, if only in a month's time, it becomes possible to take the risk of confronting them in these ways.

*   *   *

It was only after we got our regular session at the health centre that I felt I could say to Dr Hepton, 'You don't much like mental handicap, do you?' To my surprise he told me his sister had a mongol son and he had lost touch with her because of him. I was rather embarrassed; but the next time we met he asked me if I knew anything about the services in Westhampton, and we talked about how hard it is to say the right thing. I think he was surprised that I get confused too. Since then we have done several visits together and I see him quite differently.

*   *   *

Finally, if things are really rather difficult, it can be a help to involve a third party to try and straighten them out. They can ask the simple question that one dare not risk onself, can be some guarantee that reason will prevail, and can keep hope alive for a relationship for which one is oneself despairing.

Honesty, directness, regularity and a referee are not very new suggestions for better teamwork, but they are much neglected. If it sounds too much like caseworking one's colleagues, one has to ask what is casework, anyway? If you can't take your own medicine, what is the matter with it? Relationships with colleagues are too precious to be left to chance: it is important to think about them as carefully as about one's personal relationships. If that were done consistently, there would be much more strength in our services and much more room for clients.

6

Creating New Services

Social workers can do a great deal to help by making sure that existing services are publicised and do their declared job. They can do even more by treating every mentally handicapped person, and every family of a mentally handicapped person, as unique: by trying to understand the precise meaning of mental handicap for that person or family, and by finding ways of responding to their individual needs, whether through existing services or by improvisation. In most places certain needs are not being met because some element in the total pattern of service is missing. This is the starting-point for what we might call service renewal. This process should be an essential and routine part of any service system. Whatever system one builds some people will be left out of it − not from malice or stupidity, but from ordinary human blindness. If this could be accepted as a fact of life, it would perhaps be easier to make proposals for change without seeming to criticise the life's work of those who run existing services. Since it rarely is accepted, social workers must assume that change will only occur if a good case is made for it, and often only if an aggressive campaign is waged.

There are three starting-points for this process of change. One is to have a blueprint or checklist, which describes all the elements of a comprehensive service, and to review one's local services against this blueprint. A second is to examine existing services and identify the points at which they fail to meet general objectives of care for the mentally handicapped. The third is to start from the individual case, as encountered by the social worker, and draw out its lessons. Social workers have not shown themselves very adept at any of these activities in the past. Characteristically they prefer to keep their heads down in individual case material and leave it to other people to do any planning which is needed. They are not alone in this, but will remain relatively ineffectual until they broaden their horizons.

Several blueprints are circulating at present. The principal – and most poignant – one is the final publication of the National Development Group (DHSS, 1980), available free from the DHSS Store, No. 2 Site, Manchester Road, Heywood, OL10 2PZ (0706–66287). This is indeed a checklist, since it works in careful detail through each aspect of a comprehensive service. It is not, however, a checklist of *standards*, since it sets none, and they must be inferred from the questions or written in locally. It is an invaluable framework for local discussion and should be in the hands of all people concerned with comprehensive service provision. It must be said to supplement the STAMINA series, produced by the National Society for Mentally Handicapped Children and Adults. It does not greatly matter which blueprint is adopted, as any outside prescription will have to be altered for the local scene, and the process of amendment will usually generate a fruitful local discussion.

For the second starting-point, the most powerful tool is likely to be the PASS scheme of evaluating existing services. The acronym stands for Programme Analysis of Service Systems, and is one of the most thorough methods of reviewing the effectiveness of residential and day care services. Field services would also gain from a similar approach. The system was developed by the Canadian Association for the Retarded, principally for services for the mentally handicapped (although it could well be applied to other client groups) and is based on the principle of normalisation – creating services which anyone would be happy to use, and which allow maximum attention to individual need. Some may wish to argue about the theoretical base, but the detailed way in which a PASS investigation is carried out, and the scope it allows for discussion of investigators' findings, guarantee that it will be productive in most settings. There is a full-scale training programme for PASS investigators and CMH has already run some workshops in this country, and could help to suggest people who could help in this capacity. The two crucial elements, however — detailed attention to specific issues, and careful comparison and discussion of the findings of different investigators — can be built into any local review. Appendix I shows a brief version of a PASS questionnaire which appeared in the CMH ENCOR report (Thomas *et al.*, 1978).

One of the linchpins of the PASS system is Individual Programme Planning (IPP). If services are truly trying to meet the needs of individuals then it must be possible for them to record what they are aiming at; and to monitor progress towards these goals. There is nothing new in this idea, but in practice it is often lost in the pressure of daily work. IPP is also described in the ENCOR booklet, and one again senses the commitment to principles and to detail. The report mentions fifteen elements of an Individual Programme Plan:

1. Recognition of an individual rate of development, to which all planning efforts are committed.
2. The appointment of a programme co-ordinator for each individual.
3. The client and his family make the first input about their hopes and wishes.
4. The whole process is multi-disciplinary.
5. Assessment is related to reasonable, practical objectives.
6. Fully detailed long-term and short-term goals are stated.
7. These are given time limits, and put into a chronological order.
8. Understandable language is used.
9. Measurable objectives are chosen.
10. The methods of intervention are specified.
11. Specific responsibilities are laid on individual people and agencies.
12. The effectiveness of intervention is monitored.
13. Barriers to achievement are taken seriously.
14. The programme is reviewed quarterly.
15. The whole process is thus self-correcting.

Such a programme makes it possible to review the progress of individual clients; but it also makes it possible to identify (point 13) gaps or inadequacies in existing services.

And so the two processes come together. Every case makes a comment on the existing services. Of course no one comment is enough. Caseloads vary so much that social workers are diffident about making generalisations: their sample is very small and often highly skewed. But this is no reason for failing to record the evidence and to collect the comments. Over time the record does begin to have some balance, especially if it is collated with the record of other people's caseloads. One begins to notice that the parents of children at one particular special school regularly complain about transport arrangements, or that GPs in one particular town never refer to the assessment clinic, or that the patients of one particular paediatrician are more often angry about the way the news of their baby's handicap was broken to them. It is not good enough to hope that such impressions will simply build up in the memory and surface at the right moment: some may, but most will not. What is needed is a way of recording clear statements about what should happen in particular cases and what can actually happen. The gaps revealed like this should be reported to whatever monitoring groups exist. These may include a BASW branch meeting, the committee of the local parents' association, a review group at the local mental handicap hospital, an SSD special interest group, or the joint care planning team itself. Each area will have its own pattern of such groups and it is important to find out what they are.

It is also important at this stage not to allow false loyalties to suppress the discussion. *The overriding professional loyalty for a social worker is to his or her clients.* If their needs are not being met this should be stated, even if the existing services, managements or politicians feel embarrassed. Why should they, anyway? Not all needs can be met. It is the job of managers and politicians to decide which needs should be met and which must wait; but these priorities change from time to time. There may be tactical reasons for presenting the information in particular ways or at particular times, but it should be presented. Otherwise the discussion of priorities is pre-empted.

So much for the first phase — extracting information about unmet need from current cases. The second phase, once a gap has been identified, is to produce a way of filling it. There is no special reason why planners should be left to invent new solutions for clients' problems. Specialists ought to be in the best position to know what has been tried already and what is likely to succeed. They should also know the most likely sources of information about good practices and new experiments elsewhere. Again social workers are not universally good at keeping up to date with this kind of information. Fortunately, in the field of mental handicap, there are a number of organisations which do the donkey work, and either hold information and offer an advisory service or provide regular bulletins about new developments. The Hester Adrian Research Centre is the best example of the first, and the Campaign for Mentally Handicapped People and the National Society for Mentally Handicapped Children and Adults (through *Parents' Voice*) do the second. In each area there should be at least one place in which the publications of these organisations are readily available to professionals and parents alike.

Sometimes, however, it appears that no one has managed to produce a model which fits the gap in question. It may then be necessary to experiment with new ideas locally. All good ideas start somewhere and someone has to try them out, with no guarantee of success. This is something which local voluntary societies are well placed to do with, if necessary, advice from professionals and funds from statutory sources. Characteristically, such projects often have to be started by one or two enthusiastic individuals who believe in an idea before it is generally acceptable, and push it into existence against official scepticism. However, such individuals can be found in statutory settings as well as voluntary ones; and the introduction of 'joint finance' showed that such people can be encouraged to bring their ideas out into the open, if they think there is any hope of experimenting with them.

One of the barriers to effective experimental work is the inability of most practitioners to think in administrative terms. Many good ideas are lost because they are presented in a very preliminary state, which administrators cannot readily translate into budgetary and planning terms. Having plenty to do, they simply shelve the issue or return the proposal to its originator. There is no reason why practitioners should be good at teasing out the administrative implications of their ideas. What is needed is some means of interpreting practitioners and administrators to one another. Appendix II contains a New Projects Checklist, for just this purpose. It was designed for practitioners so that they could foresee problems that were likely to occur as their proposal passed along the line. It can be used also as a formal way of presenting the proposal to administrators. (See also Anderson, 1979.)

Effective presentation and the anticipation of problems is only a first step. Often a project will be in competition with other proposals and will not readily speak for itself. The value of a working group now emerges strongly. Some innovators are able single-handed, to work out the implications of their schemes and do the necessary publicity work – arguing their merits in public and in private. A project team or working party can help to carry things forward in at least two important ways. It can allow ideas to be tackled among a number of experienced people and modified to be as likely to succeed as possible; and it can involve representatives of crucial funding or managing bodies in the early planning, so that they feel identified with the project and can reassure the bodies from which they come that it is not a hare-brained scheme. Those who propose new schemes are often unduly protective of their proposal, not wishing it to be critically tested too soon; and they miss the opportunity of having it helpfully modified at an early stage – sometimes in quite surprising ways. As a general rule it will be valuable to have a forum in which gaps in service can be discussed, possible models for new service arrangements reviewed and proposals brought to a final form.

In discussing the creation of new services, I mean to assert that this is a proper part of the social worker's function, of meeting the needs of those currently left outside established services. I have no wish to claim that this is only a social work function. Anyone concerned to help those who are in need may be the appropriate person to take a new initiative, and many such initiatives come from people who are wholly new to the field, who are seeing the problems for the first time and cannot believe that anyone could tolerate them. I am concerned, though, to help social workers to take a lead more often — to see themselves as initiators and feel responsible for winning resources for their clients.

For some social workers 'social action' is seen as a radical departure from their ordinary casework role, leading in directions which are unpredictable but which will probably involve conflicts with their own employers, colleagues in other services or local politicians. Sometimes conflict is unavoidable and it is rarely just negative. In the model of social work described on page 6, and in the example of campaigning quoted on page 85, it is clear that conflict is an accepted option — part of the repertoire — in the pursuit of legitimate professional goals. It makes an enormous difference that the social worker was not operating alone, but as the agent of a consumer group. But this is exactly what social workers should be, whoever employs them. Much of the difficulty of social work in a local authority setting is that this primary responsibility is confused by other issues — hierarchy and employment contract. A social worker who sees unmet need has a responsibility to take whatever action is necessary to eliminate it. Each social worker must decide which needs should have priority at any one time, and the views of colleagues, clients and employers will be relevant to that decision; but if new services are required and campaigning is necessary to obtain them, this is a legitimate and necessary direction for the social worker to take.

Many situations of potential conflict can be circumvented if issues can be discussed long before they are spotlighted by particular crises. A discussion of good practice is much less threatening than a discussion of bad practice. Establishing a way for those who are interested in mental handicap to meet regularly would create the right kind of forum. Some areas have meetings of the Association of Professions for the Mentally Handicapped; but many rely on occasional public gatherings organised by NSMHC, by special school parent— teacher associations or by staff at the mental handicap hospital. Where no such groups exist social workers should consider how they might get one convened, as a way of anticipating conflict and making creative relationships.

The future of the large hospital

It is not possible to write about mental handicap at the present time without referring to the central, unresolved issue of the future of large hospitals. Since the 1950s, when Russell Barton's work on institutionalisation showed that large institutions are of themselves destructive places (Barton, 1959) and since the Brooklands experiment (Tizard and Grad, 1964) showed that even with grossly handicapped and disturbed children small units could greatly advance their development, it has been clear that hospitals had to change out of all recognition. But the intrinsic attraction of segregation as a solution to the problems of peculiar people, the apparent economic advantages of large-scale operations in reducing unit costs (at least if the original capital costs are forgotten), and the greater ease with which inexperienced staff can be integrated into the service in large establishments, have all meant that the large hospital is still with us. It is true that the government has now stopped them being built; that the number of children under 16 living in them dropped from 7100 in 1969 to 3900 in 1977 (the target of the 1971 White Paper 'Better Services for the Mentally Handicapped' was 5200 by 1991!); that the government has now declared: 'We believe the time has come to state unequivocally that large hospitals do not provide a favourable environment for a child to grow up in' (DHSS, 1980); and that the paper, *Care in the Community* (DHSS, 1981) has proposed some practical ways to transfer hospital patients to local authority care. But one must notice that most of the children not admitted to hospital have simply been left at home, since the number of places in residential homes for mentally handicapped children has only risen by 500. It is true that the number of adults dropped over the same period from 49,200 to 44,100 (1991 target – 27,300), and that places in residential homes for mentally handicapped adults increased from 4200 to 11,700 (1991 target – 30,000), but the government is still very equivocal about the role of the mental handicap hospitals. All it felt able to say in the 1980 DHSS report was that the assumption that there are some mentally handicapped people who need hospital care 'cannot go unchallenged', and that it would be 'desirable to give further thought to the balance between health and local authority provision'.

The Jay Report (1979) came out unequivocally for the provision of residential accommodation for mentally handicapped people not in large hospitals but in small neighbourhood units; but it frightened the government with its estimate of the increased number of staff needed to run such units, and the nursing profession by its proposal to place responsibility for the training of all mental handicap residential care staff on the Central Council for Education and Training in Social Work (CCETSW). It will be a tragedy if discussion of the Report becomes locked only in considerations of economics and vested interest; though it will clearly have to run the gauntlet of such considerations.

The Jay Committee was not asked to make recommendations about the administrative structure of services for mentally handicapped people. It was not, therefore, in a position to suggest changes in the responsibility of the National Health Service or SSDs. It set out for itself, however, a number of principles which should inform any service for mentally handicapped people; on the basis of these proposed a model structure for service; and then, in the light of that model, considered the nature of the caring task with mentally handicapped people 'without being constrained by how that task is currently allocated between particular professions or agencies'. Strictly speaking, therefore, Jay is not about transferring mentally handicapped people from hospital to local authority care, although it is often presented in this way. In theory it leaves open the question as to which authority should plan and run residential services for mentally handicapped people. It would be naive, however, not to recognise that the impetus of the Committee's recommendation that the CCETSW should control training for all residential staff in this field, is towards making residential services a responsibility of local government. This structural issue could so easily be swamped by other considerations that it must not be allowed to dominate the more buoyant first principles proposed by the Committee (para. 91):

1. Mentally handicapped children should be able to live with a family.

2. Any mentally handicapped adult who wishes to leave his or her parental home should have the opportunity to do so.
3. Any accommodation provided for adults or children should allow the individual to live as a member of a small group.
4. If they so wish, mentally handicapped people should be able to live with their peers who are not mentally handicapped.
5. Staffed accommodation should wherever possible be provided in suitably adapted houses which are physically integrated with the community.
6. These houses should be as local as possible to help the handicapped person to retain contact with his own family and community.
7. Mentally handicapped people should be able to live in a mixed sex environment.
8. Mentally handicapped people should be able to develop a daily routine like other people.
9. There should be a proper separation of home, work and recreation.

The actual model of care proposed by the Jay Committee does not sound revolutionary: mostly it draws together familiar structures. The members of the Committee confess to having had difficulty themselves in eliminating conventional ideas about the way things work at present, while trying to imagine a new way of working in the future. Their problem was in part that they were not proposing wholly new structures, but new attitudes within existing structures, new uses for familiar structures, and somewhat different structures. What, then, is the Jay argument about? First, it is about whether any mentally handicapped people need to be cared for in hospital — not for physical conditions or temporary illnesses, but because of their mental handicap itself. Second, on the assumption that large institutions, serving whole health districts, are an unsatisfactory way of providing long-term care for mentally handicapped people, it is about how one can move from dependence on such structures to a more flexible, local and integrated form of care. Third, in so far as these more local units need staff, it is about how people can best be attracted and prepared for such work, including those who are already engaged in it.

This argument is largely about means rather than ends. As the personal reservations at the end of the Jay Report make clear, there is a very wide consensus that services should be organised on a more local, and more individual, basis. Those who were opposed to the recommendation that training should be organised by the CCETSW, did so, either on the grounds that mentally handicapped, and particularly severely mentally handicapped people required an independent service of their own, or that local authorities could not be trusted to give high enough priority to them, among their many other duties, nor to achieve high enough standards for the staff they employed.

It is certainly very important to recognise the danger of polarising the argument by referring only to the worst hospitals of the past, and the most enlighted possible local authorities in the future. We are very conscious now of the dangers of institutional care, and want very badly to believe that more humane forms of care can be provided. However, it is by no means clear that all local authorities would respond as positively as would be required, if large hospitals were to be closed within a reasonably short period. Some would not release enough resources to set up hostels for those who need them; others would set up hostels, but with inadequately trained staff; others again would provide hostels, but not for the most severely handicapped people. It takes a very determined and principled local authority to accept responsibility for the most disabled people, when it cannot meet its responsibilities to others for whom the public shouts louder, and with whom councillors can identify more easily.

It is for this reason that there is ambivalence, to say the least, among some parents about the possible run-down of hospitals. At present the hospitals represent a kind of ear-marking of funds, however inadequate, for mentally handicapped people. If these funds are transferred from the NHS to local authorities with no earmarking, how can parents be sure that they will not be transferred to the elderly or to child care, with the next swing of public sympathy? So long as local government has any autonomy, this will remain a danger. On the other hand, there is the possibility of winning more resources by a swing of public sympathy towards mentally handicapped people. And the record of local government in special education has generally been a good one, since it took over from the NHS in 1971. There is a real sense in which the philosophy of 1971 needs to be extended to adult groups: education should take pride of place from treatment; and the role of carers should include that of teacher. It is not, therefore, in any polemical spirit that I suggest that social workers should take their lead from the Jay Report, and lend their knowledge and experience to the detailed task of rebuilding the residential service.

Some people are still unconvinced that the most severely handicapped people can be cared for outside the large institution. But there is a growing body of evidence from all over the world that this is possible. The message of Brooklands was that some of the most grossly disturbed and handicapped children could be contained in a small local unit, and could be given a real chance of development towards independence. A similar demonstration is now being made by the Spastics Society at Beechtree House, near Royston in Hertfordshire. In the Wessex Health Area, Dr Albert Kushlick has gradually distributed a network of small units in the community, with similar results for adults. The East Nebraska Community Office of Retardation (ENCOR) has shown that it is possible to create a network of accommodation in the community, which can not only receive some of the most severely and multiply handicapped people from existing mental handicap hospitals, but can prevent future admission to hospital completely. Between 1970 and 1977 the population from East Nebraska in their state hospital, Beatrice State Institution, fell from 550 to 290, and the waiting list from 40 to nil (Thomas *et al.*, 1978, p. 17). Admissions to the State Institution, which had previously been about ten per year, ceased in 1974. The ENCOR report is perhaps the most exciting document available for people wishing to recast the future of services in Britain.

It is clear from these programmes and others that very many, if not all, patients at present in hospital could be cared for in smaller units, providing a more normal domestic atmosphere, closer to ordinary community life, such as traffic and shops and neighbours; that they would benefit from this extension of their experience; and that the community would also benefit from knowing of their existence in a real and not a phantasied way. This must be the goal for all those people who do not have active medical conditions which demand constant access to specialised hospital equipment and services.

How is this to be achieved, and what role should social workers be playing in the campaign? As so often in this book, one has to say that this is not a matter for separate disciplines. Social workers should be found at the heart of any battle for individual liberty and opportunity. They should be able to advise on the best ways of implanting a new hostel into a community, of helping a group of patients to prepare themselves for more independence, or of setting them up in a flat. But these are not tasks specific to social work, and not all social workers are especially good at them. Social workers should also − ideally − be effective resource-winners, and in particular should know how to make their own employers play an effective part in creating new facilities. Again, this cannot be assumed. Social workers should ask themselves, in the context of their local services:

− What stage has the campaign reached here?
− Is it accepted that too many people are still in large institutions? If not, how can the evidence be brought home?
− If so, what resources are needed, to create alternative living arrangements? What kind of facility will be needed, and which should be the first to be established?
− Whose agreement will be needed for this? What money? What staff? Who will control it? Where is the best forum for planning the campaign to win these things?
− How can people at present in the hospitals be selected and prepared for more independent living?
− What evidence do I have, from the people known to me, of unused human potential?
− What is the best thing for me to do, given my abilities and the needs of the situation?

This whole process is very complex, and the ways in which

public opinion moves are very mysterious. It is important to keep an historical perspective, and recognise that many of the same hospital staff, who are in some danger of being cast in the role of obstructors of the new movement, are in fact the people who have carried the burden of care through a long period of pessimism and frustration. Ten years ago it was they – or at least some of them – who tried to interest local authorities in the provision of hostel accommodation and foster care; who reported on the lessons of Brooklands and Wessex; and experimented with behaviour modification. It does them an injustice to point only to the failures of the hospital system; loses important allies for the process of change if they are thrown only on to the defensive; and conjures false expectations for the future if it is assumed that structural changes alone will alter living experience.

But the experience of the hospitals need never be repeated. Even the best hospitals are characterised by behaviour which they themselves produce: groups of patients walking round the grounds hand in hand; patients on the wards who importune every visitor, because they see relatively few, and attach personal importance to none; patients whose pockets bulge because they cannot leave their belongings anywhere safely; others who are instinctively hostile because they only experience other disturbed patients who intrude on them. These tell-tale signs are a by-product of keeping a lot of people together in a place far from their friends and relatives, and isolated from ordinary human transactions. They do not witness to cruelty and neglect, but to concentration on certain needs at the expense of others. It is easy now to be wise about that expense, but much less easy to calculate the price we shall have to pay for what we are now planning to do.

Let us try to do that for a moment, however. Suppose that the hospitals were run down: what would be the outcome? It is easy to spot the first price to be paid: more families would keep their mentally handicapped sons and daughters at home. This shift has already occurred with children; it is probably happening with a number of people who used to have short-term care in hospitals; and, in the future, it may also happen with adults who need residential care. This is not necessarily a bad thing. It is possible that public sympathy has swung sufficiently for families to feel better supported by friends and neighbours. It may be that additional financial support from the government has made it economically easier to keep a handicapped person at home. Perhaps the primary care professionals are more sensitive to the needs of such families. The trouble is that these conditions are so hard to check once patients are dispersed, or if they have never been admitted. It is much harder to send a health advisory service team – or indeed a BBC cameraman – into twenty-five private houses than into a ward, so the real price goes unknown.

A second price will be paid by foster-parents and landladies, who receive mentally handicapped people into their homes. Perhaps one needs to worry less about them, because they will have accepted their role freely, will be recompensed for it, and can opt out of it. Nevertheless, some will have bitten off more than they can chew, or will find themselves with less than the support they need. What is more important, mentally handicapped people placed with foster-parents or landladies are in a very vulnerable position. It is true that they have access to a much more 'normal' lifestyle than that of the hospital, but it is also a much more private, secret one, which outsiders cannot readily investigate. A proper deal on this would mean a full-scale support system for the householders, which would also supply help to residents in their development towards self-care. This role has been well described; but can it be assumed that appropriate posts will be created – and sustained through the next round of cuts? The sad history of the Brighton boarding houses to which mentally handicapped patients were discharged is the clearest warning.

Third, and similarly, a price will be paid by those mentally handicapped people who live in group homes, or individual flats and bed-sitters. They will pay a price in loneliness and anxiety; some will pay a price in hunger and squalor; others in teasing and rejection. It may be worth this to them to have their own front door key and freedom to make choices; but they too will be vulnerable and hidden, unless someone seeks them out. Again, there is no problem about how to do this: there is a question about the will. These people will be living on the margins of independence and dependence. We know from experience that the border patrols tend to vanish when pressure builds up elsewhere — when newspapers scream about child abuse, or the juvenile crime figures soar; or geriatric wards run short of nurses for the internal rota. Then the community visitors simply stop calling, and the supervision ceases. It is all too easy, because responsibility is shared, and rarely comes to roost on the shoulders of any one person.

Finally, there will be a cost to be met by the staff and residents in hostels. Staffed hostels seem to be the right kind of compromise. From 1971 onwards they were the one kind of facility which local authority SSDs were ready to build (though few found the money) for mentally handicapped people: twenty-four places, residents attending the ATC during the day-time, maybe a self-contained flat for four at one end. Not a big institution, but supplied with regular support. No problems! But a hostel of twenty-four places is still very large: it stands out in its neighbourhood like a mansion. Even twelve or ten places needs an unusual building. And with the usual turnover of residents, staff remain in control: they have to, to ensure that cleaning, cooking, meal-times and gardening are all properly organised. The staff any-way are numerous enough to be hard to keep tabs on, and they change. And when a hinge comes off a door the treasurer's rules say that a particular tradesman has to deal with it, who tends to be rather slow. Pets are not allowed, and you cannot take outside friends to your room. In all sorts of little ways, the strangeness of the residents' situation is brought home to them still. It is clear from the experience of old people's homes and children's homes, and has been etched on the brain by Miller and Gwynne (1973) that the cancer of institutional-isation can appear in any situation where one group of people has power over another group.

So, let us beware any discussion in which it is assumed that changing the form of a service will, of itself, alter the content. It is close to the heart of social work to watch out for people whose needs are not met by the system they are caught up in: it is, therefore, appropriate for social workers to listen to individuals, and speak out for them; to insist on their partici-pating in reviewing their own present, and in planning for their own future; and to support whatever other arrangements they wish to have made for advocacy of their interests. This is as necessary for those living in hostels and group homes as it is for those living in hospitals: they are caught up in a new system, with new opportunities and new dangers. If society becomes more attuned to their special needs, then it may be possible for the attention of social workers to move to other groups — normalisation will have occurred.

In the meantime, social workers must be critical of their own services, and be willing to submit them to scrutiny by parents' groups, by PASS investigators, by personal advocates, and by colleagues in other services. It is only by behaving as they would like others to behave, when they are running institutions and organisations themselves, that social workers can justify their claim to patrol the boundaries on behalf of those who get trapped outside them.

Appendix I

PASS Questionnaire*

A system of helping services is simply no stronger than the systems to monitor its quality. But what to look for – that's the question.

Training as a PASS rater involves a lengthy process. It's well worth it because one's approach to human services will never be quite the same after PASS. The purpose here, though, is to focus on the attitudes and observations imbedded in this evaluation tool. While complex, PASS leads the advocate to ask questions which often boil down to the simple maxim of whether a person would want to be treated in the same way.

ASK YOURSELF THESE QUESTIONS ABOUT OUR HOSTELS, HOUSES AND SERVICES

INTEGRATION – to take part in the mainstream. To be accepted by peers.

Size or dispersal
1. Are there so many handicapped persons being served that the surrounding community is not able to accept them?
2. Is the number of people served in a residence so large that the people don't go outside for their personal relationships?

Program and facility labels
1. Does the sign outside tell that the people inside are 'different'?
2. Would the labels produce a negative or hopeless feeling among most people?

Social opportunities
1. Does the handicapped person interact with non-handicapped persons where he lives? Where he works or goes to school? In his free time? When he shops, attends church, and the like?

AGE APPROPRIATE STRUCTURES – to be valued by others as a true peer.

Facilities, design and decorations
1. Is the facility, the design of the facility and wall decorations

---

*A WALK THROUGH PASS (Programme Analysis of Service Systems).
Drawn up by Greater Omaha Association for Retarded Citizens.

appropriate for the age of the persons being served? Are adults living or working in child-like settings?

Possessions

1. Are the possessions owned by the handicapped person appropriate to his age? Does what an adult owns make him appear child-like?
2. Are attempts being made by staff to encourage their clients to own age appropriate possessions?
3. Is there appropriate space where a person lives for the possessions he owns?

Labels and forms of address

1. Are handicapped adults addressed as though they were children? Is a child-like nickname used, such as Tommy or Bobby?
2. Are labels such as kid, child, youngster used when referring to a handicapped adult?
3. Does the staff use a tone of voice with handicapped adults that would be used with children?

Activities and routines

1. Are handicapped persons engaged in activities that are appropriate for their age? Do adults work during the day? Is a child's school session limited to two hours?
2. Are the daily routines of handicapped persons typical and age appropriate? Is an adult given a coffee break — or is it recess? Is a nap scheduled during a child's school day?

Autonomy (self direction) and rights

1. Are handicapped persons given a chance to make input into decisions regarding their lives? Who makes the decisions in a person's life?
2. Are handicapped persons assisted in becoming independent rather than dependent? Will he need just as much support six months from now?
3. Do handicapped persons exercise more rights as they grow older?
4. Are handicapped persons encouraged to exercise their rights, such as voting or privacy?
5. Are rights removed only when there has been a determination of reduced competency in the area to be limited? Is the restricting of a person's rights used only as a last resort? Are there other alternatives?

Sex behaviour

1. Do handicapped persons interact with the opposite sex? Are they given time alone?
2. Are handicapped persons given support to understand their sexual identity? As a life-long process, does it begin at an early age?
3. Is counselling available to handicapped adults who may need assistance about dating, marriage, and birth control?

Personal appearance
1. How typical of his age is a handicapped person's hair style and clothing? Are there subtle mannerisms that make him look different than his peers?

CULTURE APPROPRIATE STRUCTURES — to know and respond to local customs.

Labels and forms of address
1. Are labels or forms of address used for handicapped persons which are demeaning, devaluing and implying inferiority? Does the form of address show the person to be valued as an equal?
2. Are handicapped persons labelled by their diagnosis, such as 'he is an epileptic' or 'he is a retardate'?
3. Are courtesy and respect towards handicapped persons lacking when staff talk to them?
4. In his presence, is a handicapped person talked about as a third party? Does the conversation go on as if he were not there?

Personal appearance
1. Are staff committed to correct physical defects which make a person look different?
2. What is being done to help handicapped persons with bizarre mannerisms such as self-mutilation, extreme destructiveness, and repetitive behaviours? Do these measures work? Is there a persistent and creative attempt to try again?

SPECIALIZATION — to meet the needs of each person at his particular stage of growth.

1. Is the program designed to meet the specific needs of every handicapped person?
2. As needs change, how does the program change?
3. Is a person regressing because he does not fit into the group by reason of his age, ability or behaviour?
4. Is the activity being done in an appropriate setting under the right need?
5. Does the staff have what it takes in skills and attitudes to meet the specific needs?

DEVELOPMENT GROWTH — to enable a person to learn at his own pace.

Physical overprotection
1. Are physical features built into the facility to prevent handicapped persons' movement?
2. How are situations involving risk used to prompt growth?

Social overprotection
1. Is control so emphasized or challenging opportunities so lacking that an individual's growth is restricted?
2. Are there some rules in the program that non-handicapped people would not tolerate?

3. Are handicapped persons denied new experience because 'they are unable to handle them'?

Intensity of programming

1. Is there a conviction among the staff that handicapped people are growing? Do their records prove growth is taking place?
2. Is the teaching effort organized? Does it push people to their potential?
3. When growth is stalled, where is the responsibility placed – on the person's handicap or the staff's lack of creativity?

QUALITY OF SETTING – to create an atmosphere where a person feels comfortable and accepted.

Physical comfort

1. Is the furniture and physical environment comfortable?
2. Is the temperature controlled? Is it quiet? Do the people like the food?
3. If a home, does it have a 'lived-in' quality?
4. 'Would *I* feel comfortable if I worked or lived in this place?'

Environmental beauty

1. Has attention been paid to the appearance of the surroundings? Do the efforts show good taste? What about details?
2. 'Is this place pleasing enough to have my family live there?'

Individualization

1. What evidence is there that people are encouraged to express themselves in their own way?
2. Is there a place where a person can be alone?
3. Do people usually do things as a group?
4. Do the individualized program plans reflect the differences in people?
5. Is it evident that staff appreciate individuals as having their own rich personality?

Interactions

1. What interaction is going on between clients, staff and the public? Is it warm, or cold and distant?
2. Are there individual friends among staff and clients? Are people listened to?
3. Who seems left out?
4. 'Would I be happy here?'

Training as a PASS investigator is available in the United Kingdom through the CMH Education and Research Association, 10 Fitzroy Square, London W1P 5HQ.

Appendix II

New Projects Checklist

NAME OF PROJECT
OBJECT (client/age group; type of service; full-time/part-time; short-term/long-term; who else involved?)
PROJECT CO-ORDINATOR
RESOURCES NEEDED:
1. *Property*
   Is a site or building needed?   Is one identified?
   If so, what is it?
   Address.
   Name and address of owner.
   Purchase or lease required?   Is the owner willing?
   Are alterations needed?   If so, what?
   When would it be available?   For how long?
   Is car parking needed?   Is this available?
   Is the building supervised?   Who will hold the key?
   Have the following been consulted: architect/solicitor/fire preven-
      tion officer/planning officer?
2. *Furniture and equipment*
   Is the building adequately furnished?
   If not, what is needed: (a) for ordinary purposes
                           (b) for catering purposes
                           (c) for special programmes?
3. *Staff*
   Title of each post.
   Full-time/no. of hours.
   Grading/volunteer.
   Is it an existing post?
   Holder/person to be appointed.
   Name of person who will be operationally responsible.
4. *Finance*
   What will the project cost to set up:
   (a) for purchase of land and/or building
   (b) for furniture and equipment, fixed and loose
   (c) for other needs?

What will the running costs be:
(a) for rent or loan charges
(b) for maintenance of premises
(c) for rates, heating, lighting, furniture and equipment
(d) for telephone
(e) for cleaner/caretaker (if not staff post)
(f) for transport
(g) for staff posts
(h) for other needs?
What income will be realised:
(a) through grants
(b) through donations
(c) through charges for service?
Will the project result in savings elsewhere?   How much?
Has budget provision been made?
If not, what is the source of finance (savings in budget, external
    funds, development in next budget)?
Will the project be evaluated?   By whom?
List similar projects.
Relevant written material.
What authority is needed for the project?
What time-table must be followed?

Remember

— Someone will have to answer these questions.
— Do not just assume that other people have the time.
— Other people's answers may not be favourable to you.
— You probably do not know all the answers.
— Asking others to help you will get a better response than
  dumping the problem on them.
— If questions are unanswered, the project will slow down or die.

Bibliography

A fuller and categorised bibliography, including a list of journals relevant to mental handicap, has been deposited with the library of the National Institute for Social Work, Mary Ward House, 5–7 Tavistcock Place, London WC1H 9FS.

*   *   *

Adams, M. and Lovejoy, H. (1972) *The Mentally Subnormal – Social Work Approaches*, London, Heinemann.

Anderson, D. (1979) 'Enabling practitioners to contribute to practice', *Social Work Today*, 12 June.

Astell-Burt, C. (1981) *Puppetry for the Mentally Handicapped*, New York, Souvenir.

Atkinson, D. (1981) 'Simple steps to meet hidden needs', *Social Work Today*, 3 March.

Balint, M. (1964) *The Doctor, His Patient and the Illness*, London, Tavistock.

Barton, R. (1959) *Institutional Neurosis*, London, John Wright.

Bayley, M. (1973) *Mental Handicap and Community Care*, London, Routledge & Kegan Paul.

Better Services for the Mentally Handicapped (1971) Cmnd 4683, London, HMSO.

Brinkworth, R. (1979) *Improving Babies with Down's Syndrome*, London, NSMHC and Souvenir.

British Association of Social Workers (1977) *The Social Work Task*, Birmingham, BASW.

Candy, A. (1976) *A Long Way to Manhood*, London, NSMHC.

Cardiff University's Social Services (1976) *Group Home Special Report*.

Carr, J. (1975) *Young Children with Down's Syndrome*, London, Butterworth.

Carr, J. (1980) *Helping Your Handicapped Child*, Harmondsworth, Penguin.

Clark, A. D. and Clark, A. M. (1974) *Mental Deficiency: the Changing Outlook*, London, Methuen.

Clark, A. D. and Clark, A. M. (1978) *Readings from Mental Deficiency*, London, Methuen.

Collins, M. and Collins, D. (1976) *Kith and Kids*, London, Souvenir.
Cotton, M. (1981) *Out of Doors with the Handicapped*, London, Souvenir.
Craft, A. and Craft, M. (1978) *Sex and Mental Handicap*, London, Routledge & Kegan Paul.
Craft, A. and Craft, M. (1979) *Handicapped Married Couples*, London, Routledge & Kegan Paul.
Craig, M. (1979) *Blessings*, London, Hodder & Stoughton.
Cunningham, C. (1981) *Down's Syndrome – an Introduction for Parents*, London, Souvenir.
Cunningham, C. and Jeffree, D. (1971) *Working with Parents*, London, NSMHC.
Cunningham, C. and Sloper, P. (1978) *Helping Your Handicapped Baby*, London, Souvenir.
Deacon, J. (1974) *Tongue Tied*, London, NSMHC.
DHSS (1980) *Mental Handicap – Progress, Problems and Priorities*.
DHSS (1981) *Care in the Community*.
Dutton, G. (1975) *Mental Handicap*, London, Butterworth.
Eden, D. J. (1976) *Mental Handicap – an Introduction*, London, Allen & Unwin.
Edgerton, R. (1967) *The Cloak of Competence*, University of California Press.
Edgerton, R. (1980) *Mental Retardation*, London, Fontana.
Ely Hospital Enquiry (1969) Cmnd 3975, London, HMSO.
Employment Services Agency (1976) *Employing Someone Who is Mentally Handicapped* (leaflet).
ENCOR (East Nebraska Community Office of Retardation): see Thomas *et al.* (1978).
Exodus (1979) *Residential Care of Mentally Handicapped Children – the Case for Jay*.
Frenais, M. la (1971) *Language Stimulus and Retarded Children*, London, NSMHC.
Gold, M. (1968) 'Preworkshop skills for the trainable – a sequential technique', *Education and Training of the Mentally Retarded*, vol. 3, no. 1.
Gold, M. (1973) 'Factors affecting production by the retarded', *Mental Retardation*, vol. 11, no. 6.
Gold, M. (1973) 'Research in vocational rehabilitation of the retarded', in N. Ellis (ed.) *International Review of Research in Mental Retardation*, New York, Academic Press.
Gold, M. (1975) 'Vocational training', in J. Wortis (ed.) *Mental Retardation and Developmental Disabilities*, vol. 7, New York, Brunner Mazel.
Gold, M. and Scott, K. (1971) 'Discrimination learning', in W. Stephens (ed.) *Training the Developmentally Young*, New York, John Day.
Green, M. (1966) *Elizabeth – a Mentally Handicapped Daughter*, London, Hodder & Stoughton.

Greengross, W. (1976) *Entitled to Love*, London, Malaby.

Hales, A. (1978) *The Children of Skylark Ward*, Cambridge University Press.

Hannam, C. (1975) *Parents and Mentally Handicapped Children*, Harmondsworth, Penguin.

Hanvey, C. (1981) *Social Work with Mentally Handicapped People*, London, Heinemann.

Hunt, N. (1967) *The World of Nigel Hunt*, Beaconsfield, Darwen Finlayson.

Hutchinson, R. C. (1964) *A Child Possessed*, London, Maxwell Joseph (republished 1977).

Jackson, C. (n.d.) *They Say My Child is Backward*, London, NSMHC.

James, N. (1975) *Love* (publisher unknown).

Jay Report (1979) *Committee of Enquiry into Mental Handicap Nursing and Care*, Cmnd 7468, London, HMSO.

Jeffree, D. and McConkey, R. (1976) *Let Me Speak*, London, Souvenir.

Jeffree, D., McConkey, R. and Hewson, S. (1977) *Let Me Play*, London, Souvenir.

Johnson, V. and Werner, R. (1980) *Step-by-Step Learning Guide for Retarded Infants and Children*, London, Constable.

Johnson, V. and Werner, R. (1980) *Step-by-Step Learning Guide for Older Retarded Children*, London, Constable.

Jones, A. (1976) *Two to One*, London, Interaction.

Jones, M. (1968) *Beyond the Therapeutic Community*, Connecticut, Yale University Press.

Jones, M. (1976) *Maturation of the Therapeutic Community*, New York, Human Sciences Press.

Jones, P. (1979) *Mental Handicap Register – does Wandsworth need one?*, London, Wandsworth Social Services Dept.

Kings Fund (1979) *An Ordinary Life*, London, Kings Fund Centre.

Kings Fund (n.d.) *Adult Education for Mentally Handicapped People*, London, Kings Fund Centre.

Kith and Kids (1970) *One to One* (publisher unknown).

Kushlick, A. (1967) 'The Wessex experiment', *British Hospital Journal and Social Services Review*, 6 October.

Kushlick, A. and Cox, (1970) 'Planning services for the subnormal in Wessex', in Wing and Bransby (eds), *Psychiatric Case Registers*, Dept of Health Statistical Report, series 8, London, HMSO.

Lane, D. (1980) *The Work Needs of Mentally Handicapped Adults*, London, Disability Alliance.

Larsen, H. (1974) *Don't Forget Tom*, London, A. & C. Black.

Leeming, K., Swann, W., Coupe, J. and Mittler, P. (1980) *Teaching Language Communication to the Mentally Handicapped*, London, Methuen.

Livock, P. (1981) *Sex Education for the Mentally Handicapped*, London, Croom Helm.

McConkey, R. and Jeffree, D. (1981) *Let's Make Toys*, London, Souvenir.

McCormack, M. (1978) *A Mentally Handicapped Child in the Family*, London, Constable.

McCormack, M. (1979) *Away From Home – the Mentally Handicapped Child in Residential Care*, London, Constable.

McCullough, C. (1978) *Tim*, London, Pan.

Mannoni, M. (1973) *The Retarded Child and the Mother*, London, Tavistock.

Mattinson, J. (1970) *Marriage and Mental Handicap*, London, Duckworth.

Menzies, I. (1960) 'A case study in the functioning of social systems as a defence against anxiety', *Human Relations*, no. 13.

Meyers, R. (1979) *Like Normal People*, London, Souvenir.

Miller, E. and Gwynne, G. (1972) *A Life Apart*, London, Tavistock.

MIND (1972) *Your Mongol Baby*, London, MIND.

Mittler, P. (ed.) (1977) *Research to Practice in Mental Retardation*, Baltimore, University Park Press.

Mittler, P. (ed.) (1979) *People Not Patients*, London, Methuen.

Mittler, P. and Gittins, S. (eds) (1976) *The Educational Needs of Mentally Handicapped Adults*, London, NSMHC.

Morton, J. (1979) 'Four Mentally Handicapped Teenagers in Transition', unpublished (Rees Thomas School, Hawthorn Way, Cambridge).

Mussett, H. (1975) *Untrodden Ways*, London, Gollancz.

National Development Group for the Mentally Handicapped (pamphlets):
(1976) *Planning Together*;
(1977a) *Mentally Handicapped Children*;
(1977b) *Helping Mentally Handicapped School Leavers*;
(1977c) *Residential Short-term Care for Mentally Handicapped People*;
(1977d) *Day Services for Mentally Handicapped Adults*;
(1978) *Helping Mentally Handicapped People in Hospital*;
(1980) *Improving the Quality of Services for Mentally Handicapped People – a Checklist of Standards*.
London, DHSS.

Newson, J., Newson, E., Head, J. and Magford, K. (1979) *Toys and Playthings in Development and Remediation*, Harmondsworth, Penguin.

Nichols, P. (1967) *A Day in the Death of Joe Egg*, London, Faber.

Nirje, B. (1970) 'The normalisation principle', *Journal of Mental Subnormality*, vol. XVI, pt. 2, no. 31, December.

Norris, D. (1975) *Day Care and Severe Handicap*, London, NSMHC.

Office of Health Economics (1978) *Mental Handicap – Ways Forward*, London.

Oswin, M. (1971) *The Empty Hours*, Harmondsworth, Penguin.

Oswin, M. (1978) *Children Living in Long-stay Hospitals*, London, Heinemann.

Oswin, M. (1981) *Issues and Principles in the Development of Short-term Residential Care for Mentally Handicapped Children*, London, Kings Fund Centre.

Owens, G. and Birchenall, P. (1979) *Mental Handicap – the Social Dimensions*, London, Pitman.

Palmer, J. (1980) 'No pity please – my son has love', *Parents' Voice*, June.

Perkins, E. *et al.* (1971) *Helping the Retarded – a Systematic Behavioural Approach*, London, Institute of Mental Subnormality.

Poteet, J. (1974) *Behaviour Modification – a Practical Guide for Teachers*, University of London.

Purser, A. (1981) *You and Your Handicapped Child*, London, Allen & Unwin.

Rao, B. and Lockyer, D. (1979) 'Public acceptance of community care for the mentally handicapped', *Apex*, no. 7.

Ryan, J. and Thomas, F. (1980) *The Politics of Mental Handicap*, Harmøndsworth, Penguin.

Satterthwaite, J. (n.d.) *Roy and the Chocolate Box* (publisher unknown).

Seed, P. (1981) *Mental Handicap – Who Helps in Rural and Remote Communities?*, Tunbridge Wells, Costello.

Segal, R. (1970) *Mental Retardation and Social Action*, Springfield, Ill., Charles Thomas.

Shearer, A. (1972) *Our Life*, London, Campaign for Mentally Handicapped People.

Shearer, A. (1973) *Listen*, London, Campaign for Mentally Handicapped People.

Shearer, A. (1975) *No Place Like Home*, London, Campaign for Mentally Handicapped People.

Shearer, A. (1980) *Handicapped Children in Residential Care*, London, Bedford Square Press.

Shearer, M. and Shearer, D. (1972) 'The Portage Project – a model for early childhood education', *Exceptional Children*, vol. 39, p. 210.

Shennan, V. (1980) *Mental Handicap Nursing and Care*, London, Souvenir.

Smith, W. (1975) *Judith – Teaching Our Mongol Baby*, London, NSMHC.

Smithson, M. (1977) *Lesley – the Child We Chose*, London, NSMHC.

Sobol, H. (1978) *My Brother Steven is Retarded*, London, Gollancz.

Solly, K. (1972) *The Different Baby*, London, NSMHC.

Stephen, E. (ed.) (1970) *Residential Care for the Mentally Retarded*, Oxford, Pergamon.

Stephens, W. (ed.) (1971) *Training the Developmentally Young*, New York, John Day.

Stevens, M. (1976) *Education and Social Needs of Children with Severe Handicap*, London, Edward Arnold.

Stevens, M. (1978) *Observe – then Teach*, London, Edward Arnold.

Stone, S. and Taylor, F. (1977) *Handbook for Parents with a Handicapped Child*, London, Arrow.

Thomas, D., Kendall, A. and Firth, H. (1978) *ENCOR – A Way Ahead*, London, Campaign for Mentally Handicapped People.

156 *Bibliography*

Tizard, J. and Grad, J. (1964) *Community Services for the Mentally Handicapped*, Oxford University Press.

Tizard, J. and Grad, J. (1971) *The Mentally Handicapped and Their Families*, Oxford University Press.

Todd, F. J. (1967) *Social Work with the Mentally Subnormal*, London, Routledge & Kegan Paul.

Tuckey, L. *et al.* (1973) *Handicapped School Leavers and Their Future Education, Training and Employment*, London, National Children's Bureau.

Tyne, A. (1974) *Learning Together*, London, Campaign for Mentally Handicapped People.

Tyne, A. (1976) 'Residential provision for mentally handicapped adults', *Social Work Today*, 10 June.

Tyne, A. (1976) *Plans and Provisions for Mentally Handicapped People*, London, Campaign for Mentally Handicapped People.

Tyne, A. (1977) *Mental Handicap – Housing Need and the Law*, London, Campaign for Mentally Handicapped People.

Tyne, A. (1977) *Residential Provision for Adults Who are Mentally Handicapped*, London, Campaign for Mentally Handicapped People.

Tyne, A. (1977) *Housing for Mentally Handicapped People*, London, Campaign for Mentally Handicapped People.

Tyne, A. (1978) *Looking at Life in a Hospital, Hostel, Home or Unit*, London, Campaign for Mentally Handicapped People.

Tyne, A. (1978) *Participation by Families of Mentally Handicapped People in Policy-making and Planning*, London, Campaign for Mentally Handicapped People.

Tyne, A. (1978) *Review of Progress in Provision for Mentally Handicapped People*, London, Campaign for Mentally Handicapped People.

Tyne, A. and Gauntlett, P. (1978) *Working Out*, London, Campaign for Mentally Handicapped People.

Tyne, A. and Wertheimer, A. (1980) *Even Better Services?* London, Campaign for Mentally Handicapped People.

Van der Hoeven, J. (1978) *Slant-eyed Angel*, Gerrards Cross, Colin Smythe.

Voysey, M. (1975) *A Constant Burden*, London, Routledge & Kegan Paul.

Wandsworth Social Services Department (1976) *Project '74*, London.

Warnock Report (1978) *Special Educational Needs*, Cmnd 7212, London, HMSO.

Whelan, E. and Speake, B. (1977) *Adult Training Centres in England and Wales*, University of Manchester.

Whelan, E. and Speake, B. (1978) *Learning to Cope*, London, Souvenir.

Whelan, E. and Speake, B. (1981) *Getting to Work*, London, Souvenir.

Wilkin, D. (1979) *Caring for Mentally Handicapped Children*, London, Croom Helm.

Williams, P. (1978) *Our Mutual Handicap*, London, Campaign for Mentally Handicapped People.

Williams, P. and Shoultz, B. (1981) *We Can Speak for Ourselves*, London, Souvenir.

Willis, J. and Willis, E. (1974) *Bringing up Our Mongol Son*, London, Routledge & Kegan Paul.

Wills, D. (1971) *Spare the Rod*, Harmondsworth, Penguin.

Wing, L. (1976) *Children Apart – Autistic Children and Their Families*, London, MIND.

Wolfensberger, W. (1972) *Normalisation*, Toronto, National Institute of Mental Retardation.

Wolfensberger, W. (1977) *A Multi-Component Advocacy Protection Scheme*, Toronto, Canadian Association for the Mentally Retarded.

Wolfensberger, W. and Glenn, L. (1975) *Programme Analysis of Service Systems*, Toronto, National Institute of Mental Retardation.

Wolfensberger, W. and Zauka, H. (1973) *Citizen Advocacy*, Toronto, National Institute of Mental Retardation.

Zeaman, D. and House, B. (1963) 'Role of attention in retardate discrimination learning', in N. Ellis, *Handbook of Mental Deficiency*, New York, McGraw-Hill.

A Few Useful Addresses*

British Association of Social Workers, 16 Kent Street, Birmingham B5 6RD (021–622–3911).

Campaign for Mentally Handicapped People, 16 Fitzroy Square, London W1P 5HQ (01–387–9571).

Downs Children's Association, c/o Mr Cordukes, Quinborne Community Centre, Ridgacre Road, Birmingham B32 2TW (021–427–1374).

Hester Adrian Research Centre, University of Manchester, Oxford Road, Manchester 13 (061–273–3333).

Kings Fund Centre, 126 Albert Street, London NW1 7NF (01–267–6111).

MIND/National Association for Mental Health, 22 Harley Street, London W1N 2ED (01–637–0741).

National Development Team, DHSS, Alexander Fleming House, Elephant & Castle, London SE1 6BY (01–407–5522).

National Society for Mentally Handicapped Children and Adults, Pembridge Hall, Pembridge Square, London W2 4EP (01–229–8941).

*A more complete list is available from the library of the National Institute for Social Work, Mary Ward House, 5–7 Tavistock Place, London WC1H 9FS.

Author Index

Subject Index